IN THE TIME OF DRONES: A SHORT STORY OF LOVE, BETRAYAL AND PROGRAM MANAGEMENT

PORTER DRUCKER

Drones

PREFACE

This is a book about program management; specifically, the critical importance of leaders establishing the right operating culture if their teams are to achieve real and enduring program success.

Through the artifice of a short adventure yarn, the book highlights the common dysfunctions of all too many business cultures, especially those that have scaled up rapidly from tightly knit, highly centralized "garage shop" teams to mid-sized companies with thousands of employees. The narrative also addresses the importance of a constructive working relationship between government and industry management counterparts, one built on trust and recognition that both share the same over-arching performance goals.

Although Acme Aviation, the dysfunctional company portrayed here, is representative of many enterprises, it is a purely hypothetical and fictional construct. The characters too are composite representatives of managers found in businesses worldwide and they too are purely fictional.

Drones

6

CHAPTER ONE

Sam Wright left his furnished two-bedroom apartment in what passed as an upscale neighborhood of Victorville, an unremarkable desert city of about 150,000 sun-drenched Californians most often viewed by gamblers as they speed along the I-15 freeway between LA and Vegas. It was a few minutes before 6:00AM on a very crisp morning in early March and Sam paused for a few moments to take in a rose-tinted cloudless sky to the east before he took a deep breath of the cold, dry air, slid his 6-foot frame into the Tesla and headed west toward Adelanto.

The 10-year old Tesla Model S had been assigned to him as part of the community property settlement in his recent divorce. His ex got the late model S-Class Mercedes and their spacious home nestled in a gated community near Palmdale, a slightly larger and equally unremarkable desert town about 50 miles to the west. The trial judge had awarded her a large monthly alimony payment. Because theirs had been a marriage of 10 or more years (22 years and 2 months to be exact), Sam was now compelled by the Golden State to pay her this "support" until she either remarried or one of them died.

Equal justice before the law, California style, he observed and he winced at the memory of his ex-wife's surprise announcement after dinner over a year ago that she had "fallen in love" with his boss at work. She wanted a divorce so she could spend the rest of her life with her "soul mate." Good grief! What's a 45-year old woman doing yapping on and on about a "soul mate," he wondered? Must have something to do with menopause, he concluded. She also informed Sam that she had no intent to remarry since that would end the monthly spousal support she was "owed." How sweet was that? Fucking bitch, he answered wordlessly. The only good news in all this was that their only child, Carter, was already on his own, a 20-year old in his second year at the Air Force Academy and doing well.

As Sam turned right and headed north on I-395, he looked to his right and saw the sun was now just above the horizon, its light sparkling off a thick ground frost. It was a beautiful scene and reminded him just how much he loved the desert, especially in the calm, bracing air of early morning.

Many years before, as an F-15A pilot with the "Grim Reapers" Fighter Squadron based in the English Midlands, he had been selected to attend the Air Force Test Pilot School at nearby Edwards

AFB. After only a few months at the school, Sam realized he was very drawn to the Antelope Valley's dry climate, panoramic views and stunted, twisted flora. This attraction was not an acquired taste. You either hated it or you were a "desert rat." Sam loved it and worked very hard to finish at the top of his class so he could secure a test pilot position on a test team at Edwards following graduation. Five years later, he moved on to the Flight Test Center staff at Edwards. However, there were only so many senior leadership positions at the base and when he received an assignment to the Air Staff at the Pentagon over a decade ago, he knew it was "time to eject."

This decision had really upset his ex since Sam was just 6 years short of a 20-year retirement pension and had already been selected for early promotion to lieutenant colonel. Fortunately, she also loved the desert and had seemed happy enough until her surprise announcement blindsided him.

At this early hour, the 2-lane highway was almost empty of traffic and the Model S smoothly and quickly accelerated up to 85 mph, Sam's standard cruise speed on all major California roads. Twenty or so miles off to his left was the General Atomics site near Gray Butte where he had worked over the last decade, ever since he separated from the Air Force. He had truly enjoyed working at Gray Butte as a key member of the team that managed the complex test operations so important to both the company and the Nation. Despite the excellent company reputation he had established and the many close friendships built on the solid foundation of shared sacrifice and accomplishment, there was just no fucking way he could keep working there. How could he continue to report to the very asshole that had seduced his wife and made him a damn cuckold? In an effort to retain him, the company had offered him an excellent director level position down in San Diego but Sam knew he had to find a job somewhere else, preferably in the upper desert. His first thought was to call an old friend who now headed a local outfit called Acme Aviation.

Like General Atomics, Acme Aviation was a privately held company whose products were Remotely Piloted Aircraft or RPAs and the systems that supported their operations. Acme had been founded about 20 years earlier by two eccentric and wildly successful entrepreneurs, Horst Schwarz and his younger brother Hannes. Together, they owned a dozen or so businesses in the United States, Canada, Mexico, Germany and Australia. Their cash cows now were in the energy business, and they had become billionaires as a result of their market position in the oil and gas fracking business, now in yet another cycle of high prices. Both brothers held advanced degrees in Aeronautics from Princeton and both shared a lifelong passion for anything that flew.

Acme had grown from a handful of design engineers working out of a small hangar at the Mojave Airport to just over 2,000 employees operating at a half dozen southern California locations. After landing a large, classified US Government contract about 8 years ago, the Schwarz brothers had invested in the construction of a complex of hangars and office buildings adjacent to a brand new 8000-foot runway in the vastness of the Mojave Desert. The remote site was Sam Wright's destination this morning. Today was his first day of work with Acme and he was looking forward to a fresh start.

Sam stopped at the intersection with Highway 58 before continuing north on I-395 toward Ridgecrest. Getting hired at Acme had been a piece of cake. He had simply called the Acme President, William "Hopalong" Boyd, a retired Air Force Major General whom Sam had known for almost a quarter century and explained that he was available. Boyd had told Sam he would love to have him come aboard and that Acme had an open program management position that would be a "perfect fit." After that call, Sam had a few telephone chats with a woman from Acme's Human Resources group, submitted to a drug test at a certified clinic in Victorville and provided some biographical and security clearance information through the company's website. That was it. He didn't even know what program he would be managing since it was "highly classified." Now, he had a 7:00AM meeting with Boyd.

When Captain Wright had reported in to his Squadron at RAF Lakenheath in the United Kingdom, it was Lieutenant Colonel Bill Boyd, aka "Hopalong," who sat behind the Commander's large mahogany desk. After returning Sam's salute, the first thing Boyd growled was, "Well, do you wanna be 'Orville' or 'Wilbur?'" Pausing for just a few seconds, Sam had replied, "Well sir, 'Orville,' I guess." And that label had been with him ever since. When Sam arrived at Lakenheath, "Hopalong" had already been selected for promotion to full Colonel and Boyd left the base about 6 months later for a Central Command job where he played a key role in planning and executing one of the seemingly endless series of Middle East air campaigns.

When Wright arrived, Boyd had been concerned for some time about the quality of new pilots coming to the Squadron straight from undergraduate pilot training and F-15 upgrade training in Florida. Sam was one of three "green beans" selected by the Squadron Operations Officer to undergo a "Boyd receiving inspection." During a comprehensive 3-flight evaluation, Wright had thoroughly impressed Boyd with his aircraft systems knowledge as well as his "stick and rudder" flying skills. Boyd, whose previous assignment had been with the elite Aggressor unit at Nellis AFB, was widely viewed as the best pilot at the base and his standards were high. The other 2 "beans" Boyd evaluated did not receive passing marks.

A few months later, as a newcomer, Orville was assigned the unsought additional duty of organizing and executing an extended weekend visit by some Boeing and Raytheon bigwigs and their spouses. The Squadron had been selected to receive a coveted annual award as the outstanding air superiority unit in the Air Force. There were lunches, dinners, transportation, tours, Eagle flights, a golf outing and an awards ceremony hosted by an Air Force 4-star. Any number of things could have gone wrong, especially a Friday afternoon "Reaper Call" with spouses invited to the Squadron's ready room for this normally X-rated affair. With a lot of help from Boyd's secretary, Sam planned all this and it came off without a hitch. Again, Boyd had been highly impressed by the young captain and, as a result, 'Hopalong' had served as an informal mentor to Sam over the years, including the penning of an exceptionally strong endorsement in support of Sam's application to the Air Force Test Pilot School a few years later.

When General Boyd retired, he was the head of Air Force Legislative Liaison at the Pentagon and Horst Schwarz had hired him immediately based on Boyd's excellent reputation and firsthand working knowledge of how the various tribes within the Beltway interacted to make policy and procurement decisions. Schwarz needed to win some government contracts to help fund his revolutionary, but expensive, development efforts and felt that General Boyd could spearhead that effort. Within a few years, Boyd's hiring had paid off and Acme's government business was growing rapidly.

CHAPTER TWO

As he passed an old weather-beaten billboard, Sam started to decelerate. His Acme Human Relations contact, Ms. Lucia Lopes, had told him that shortly after passing that sign he needed to turn right on an unmarked road. She added that if he reached the small desert town of Atolia he had gone too far. About a minute later, Sam saw a road running off to his right and turned his Tesla east as he fumbled for his sunglasses and lowered the sun visor. The morning sun was precisely aligned with an unexpectedly wide and well-maintained 2-lane road. Less than a mile down the perfectly straight road, Sam saw a gate emerge through his squinted vision. It was hard to miss it despite the glare. An imposing wall ran about 100 yards on either side of a guard shack located between the two lanes. The huge STOP sign was completely unnecessary since a yellow and black striped steel barrier at least a yard high blocked any path forward.

At the gate, a young, uniformed and armed young man solemnly asked Sam to provide the name of his point of contact and his driver's license. As the guard handed back his license, the hydraulically powered barricade lowered quietly into the road and the guard deadpanned, "Welcome to Red Rock, Mr. Wright." When Sam asked for directions to the headquarters building where he was scheduled to meet Boyd in just over 20 minutes, the guard replied, "'Luscious' will meet you at the next gate which is about 10 miles down the road. She'll get you badged and escort you to your meeting with the General." When Sam asked who "Luscious" was, the guard apologized and said her real name was "Lucia Lopes," and then added, "but everyone out here at Red Rock just calls her 'Luscious.'"

Safely past the gate, Sam headed east on the ruler-straight road that kept his Tesla annoyingly aligned with the rising sun. Afraid that he would be late, he slowed below 85 mph only briefly when he saw a solitary coyote trot across the road about 100 yards ahead. Sam was surprised with the level of security he had just seen: not a flimsy parking lot style barrier but a massive steel obstacle no vehicle was going to bust through. And still a second level of security with another gate ahead.

Sam also noted that the guard referred to his old friend as "The General," but his main preoccupation was imagining what this "Luscious" woman would look like. Maybe it was a joke and she was anything but? On the phone, she had seemed very professional and he had imagined her as a rather sexless professional, probably, he guessed, about his own age. She had asked him just to call her "Lucia" when he repeatedly referred to her as "Ms. Lopes."

As the Tesla crested a small rise, Sam saw a complex of large buildings and what looked like part of a runway just to the south of the straight line he had been tracing. Just ahead he saw another gate, another striped steel barricade and a small building just to the right of the road. A very high chain link fence crowned with menacing coils of concertina wire stretched both north and south of the road as far as he could see.

At the gate, a uniformed guard, who with the exception of a ponytail of jet-black hair looked remarkably similar to the first guard, asked again for Sam's driver's license. As the guard studied the license, someone emerged from the building to the right of the road. Long dark hair and long black-stockinged legs were Sam's first impressions of the woman who walked in front of his Tesla. She wore a bright orange flight jacket, a very mini black skirt that extended only slightly below the jacket and some laced black boots that came about halfway up her shapely calves. It was quite a sight to see. Leaning toward his car's open window, she removed a black glove, extended her hand and brightly announced, "Hi Mr. Wright. I'm Lucia. Welcome to our Red Rock site." Sam noticed her painted orange-colored finger nails as he shook her warm hand and replied with an awkward "Thanks."

For the first time, Sam noticed she was wearing large reflective sunglasses and that her lipstick was almost exactly the same orange color as her flight jacket and nails. Halloween in March, Sam thought and this black and orange trick was truly a treat. He noticed that the velcro-attached leather nametag perched high on the pronounced swell of her flight jacket read "Luscious Lopes." Indeed, she was.

"Here's your visitor's badge," Luscious said. "It requires you to be escorted at all times and that's my job until we get you an official picture badge later this morning. Right now, I need you to park your car next to the golf cart over there," she added pointing to a gravel parking lot just to the east of the small building she had exited only a minute earlier. Sam took the badge, smiled and nodded.

A minute later, they were barreling along a road that winded around a maze of hangars, dish antennas, parking lots and trailer complexes. He noticed the lots were almost full and there was already a great deal of activity at Red Rock with small groups of people walking purposefully between the buildings. He also saw a few older model Acme RPAs being towed and spotted on a parking apron to the south. He was glad he had on a parka. Even at the low speed of a golf cart at its maximum velocity, it was pretty damn cold.

Back at the 2nd gate, Sam had noticed it was 6:52AM when he turned off the Tesla. He was very obsessed about being punctual. Having overcome a youthful habit of always being late, Sam was as zealous as any convert to a newly acquired behavior. As he climbed into the right seat of the golf cart, he had told Lucia he hoped they wouldn't be late. "Not a problem," she had confidently replied. "But you better hold on real tight." With that she had stomped on the accelerator. Tires squealed as the cart lurched out of the lot. He couldn't help but smile as they careened ahead. He liked this woman he concluded. Five minutes later, they braked to a hard stop in front of a one-story pale yellow metal building.

"Building 1, Headquarters!" Lucia announced. "Follow me," she shouted as she jumped out of the cart and raced up a small set of stairs before swiping her badge on a reader just to the right of the double door entrance. Sam heard the locks click open while he was still getting his briefcase from the back of the cart and barely got to the door before it locked shut. A few seconds later he was struggling to catch up with Lucia as she seemed to glide effortlessly down a long corridor. She finally stopped and after a few seconds, a little winded, Sam caught up with her. They now stood together just outside a closed door. To the right of the door was a small placard that read "Hopalong Boyd." Underneath the name it read, "President, Acme Aviation."

Lucia had unzipped her jacket and Sam could see her quite full figure now fully revealed by a very tight white sweater. With her sunglasses now removed, Sam examined her face closely for the first time and was surprised to see a lovely olive-skinned oval that actually looked more Asian than Hispanic. Lucia seemed to notice his extended look and his surprise. She smiled and said, "You've still got a minute or so to catch your breath. When you're ready we'll go in and I'll introduce you to his admin. Her name is Sue Garfield. She'll call me when you're finished with the General and I'll come pick you up. "

"Thanks for getting me here on time," Sam replied between deep breaths. "That was some inspired driving." Lucia's simple reply was a seductive smile. Ten seconds later, she swiped her badge, opened the door and they walked in together.

CHAPTER THREE

The large reception area was simply furnished. As Sam followed Lucia toward the desk at the far end, they passed two small rooms to the left. He noticed a copier in one room and a refrigerator in the other; to his right, he saw a large empty conference room through an open door.

The woman behind the desk looked at them over the frame of her tortoise shell glasses. Her dark hair had some gray highlights and was tightly wrapped in an attractive bun. As she stood to greet them, Sam noticed she was wearing a very tight suspender jeans outfit over a form fitting white blouse. The suspenders had to bend sharply around the outside of breasts that Sam immediately judged as implants given her otherwise slender figure. Or maybe there was just something in the water up here, he wondered? It was a little hard to guess Sue's age since her face, freckled and lined, looked far too old to be sitting on top of her curvaceous body. As Sam had noted grimly when he shaved that very morning, the wind, the sun and the low humidity of the desert were definitely hard on faces. Sam's hair was still dark and not yet receding but the deep lines around his greenish-brown eyes were unmistakable testimony to his many years squinting in the sun-baked Mojave.

"Sue, this is Mr. Wright. He's here for his 7:00AM meeting with the General," Lucia declared.

Sue shook Sam's hand and replied, "Good to meet you, Mr. Wright. The General is ready to see you now. Can I get you some coffee?"

"Pleasure to meet you too and yes, thanks on the coffee," Sam replied.

" How do you like it?"

" Black as my soul, Sue."

"My goodness!" she exclaimed in mock horror. "What a dark thought. I hope your soul is not really in such terrible shape. By the way, you can just call me 'Sugar.' Most folk around here don't call me 'Sue' anymore." At this point, Lucia excused herself with a reminder that she would return to escort Sam later. Sugar knocked on the office door across from her desk, leaned in and said something Sam could not quite make out, then stood out of his way, smiled and announced, "Go on in, sir. I'll be back with your coffee in a minute."

"'Orville!'" Boyd boomed as he met Sam at the door and engulfed Sam's hand in a large fleshy mitt. "It's damn good to see you. Give me your parka and have a seat there." Boyd pointed to an imposing leather chair at the head of a long dark wooden table as he hung Sam's parka on a small coat rack in the corner. Sam looked around the room.

A large, mostly clean mahogany desk supported a keyboard and two large monitors as well as a monstrously large carved wooden plaque that read MAJOR GENERAL "HOPALONG" BOYD. An American flag and another flag with two white stars on an Air Force Blue background stood guard duty behind the impressive desk. Sam had to smile. Boyd had always wanted to have it both ways. He wanted to be approachable as good old "Hopalong" but he also wanted you never to forget he was the boss.

Sam noticed a small conversation area in one corner with a dark leather sofa and some chairs surrounding a glass topped coffee table and wondered why they had not settled in there. The walls were full of mementos typical of a long illustrious military career and Sam noticed one of the wall coverings was a large, framed photograph of men and women standing in front of an F-15A Eagle. It had been given to "Hopalong" as he left his squadron commander assignment in the UK. Sam knew he was in the picture and that his signature was one of the many on the surrounding border. A large number of aircraft models were exhibited on a credenza along the sidewall. Before the divorce, Sam had an entire room of his Palmdale home decorated with similar pictures, models, coffee mugs and other "paraphernalia," and his career had been half as long as Boyd's. All of that stuff was now in storage since his Victorville apartment was too small to allow Sam the selfish indulgence of a "Yeah Me!" room.

"Good to see you too, sir," Sam replied as he stood by his chair and waited awkwardly for Boyd to hang up the parka and sit down in one of the slightly smaller chairs that lined the side of the conference table. As Boyd settled into his chair, Sam noticed that he had put on a few pounds since they had last met, a chance encounter about 5 years earlier at an annual Air Force Association symposium in Washington DC. Boyd had a prominent nose that dominated the middle of a now worn and craggy face. His hairline had receded a bit but the only white in his still thick sandy-colored head of hair was around the temples. Sam did some quick calculations and figured Boyd must now be in his late 60's. Out of habit, Sam sat down only after Boyd was seated.

"An impressive display," Sam commented as he nodded at the wall behind Boyd.

"Well, what the hell do you expect after almost 30 years on active duty, 6000 flight hours and combat in two different wars over goddamn Iraq?" Boyd answered with only a slight smile. Sam noticed that Boyd's Bronx accent was most noticeable when his language got a little salty. That was the end of the small talk.

Boyd continued, "Orville, like I told you when we chatted a while back, I think you are a perfect fit for a program management position we really need to fill. It's been open too damn long already and we're paying the price. We'll need to work on getting your Top Secret clearance transferred from GA and work the billet issue with the customer. Our security folk have already done enough to get you briefed in today at the Secret level after you in-process and get badged.

There was a soft knock on the door and Boyd growled, "Enter!" Sugar peeked in timidly and explained, "I have coffee for Mr. Wright."

"Well, come on in Sugar and give old Orville here his Starbucks stimulant," Boyd commanded. Sugar carefully placed a saucer and a 16 oz mug of steaming dark roast on top of a large Acme Aviation coaster she had placed on the table in front of Sam. Sam thanked her and when she asked the "General" if he needed anything, he replied gruffly with a curt "No thanks." She smiled and left.

Once she left, Sam took a sip and teased that he thought "Sugar" was a female label that had long ago passed from just being a tad sexist and politically incorrect to near total extinction. Boyd laughed and said he had given her that nickname after "she had some augmentation work done soon after I came to work here." He chuckled and added that she was single at the time and he suspected she was interested in her new boss and simply wanted to get his attention. Boyd added that he thought about calling her "Hooters" or "Melons" but figured that probably went too far.

Sam grinned and commented that Ms. Lopes was quite good looking with a great figure. Boyd proudly replied that he had nicknamed her too and then reminded Sam that he had been responsible for assigning him the "Orville" moniker as well. He ended this part of their conversation abruptly.

"Sam, we need to cover a few things quickly. At half past, we'll be joined by your new boss. He's the VP in charge of all our program managers. His name is Jim Bottom but he goes by 'Rock.' He's a bit of a fucking pill and I'd actually like to replace him but unfortunately giving people the boot, no matter how richly they deserve it, is a problem around here. I know I shouldn't share too much Acme dirty laundry with you during your first hours at the site but our operating culture needs some major rework, although I guess no place is perfect. Anyway, I'll just shut up now and let you figure things out as you go along but remember my door's always open and you should come VFR direct to me if 'Rock' or anyone else gets to be too much of a problem.

"Just to prepare you, Rock has all the personality of a wet rag so a lot of people have trouble reading him. He's a West Point grad, transferred to the Air Force at graduation, flew the F-16 operationally and has a test background like you. He also worked a while in a program office at Dayton. Retired as an O-6 and actually was hired here a few years before I came on board. Anyway, he's a real detail guy and I guess that ain't all bad but I want YOU, not 'Rock,' to run the program. Rock's got to learn to trust people and delegate. It's way past time.

"Orville, it turns out today's an important one here at Red Rock. Our big boss, Horst Schwarz, is flying in late this morning to host a VIP visit from our classified customer. After the VIP departs, you're invited to an informal lunch where I'll introduce you to Horst and some of the other key players here at Red Rock.

"FYI, Horst is a widower and lives with his girlfriend in Rolling Hills on the PV peninsula just a little south of LAX. He loves horses and has a stable there with some very expensive thoroughbreds. Anyway, the company keeps a few King Air's hangared at Torrance Airport and he just flies one up whenever he needs to visit us up here. We try to have a fully qualified pilot in the right seat, which really pisses him off. I actually wish it was less convenient for him to get up here and that I was left more alone to actually run the business but you can't argue with his success. That dude and his brother Hannes have made billions in a dozen or so different businesses scattered all over the world. And it's his money after all. "

"What about his brother, Hannes? Is he flying up too?" Sam interrupted.

"No, Hannes used to be a lot more involved but a combination of some health issues and other business interests have kept him mostly out of my hair over the past 5 years. Both these gents are around 80 but you'll see today that Horst really doesn't act anywhere near that old. Good DNA I guess. Anyway, you'll also meet my number two, a fella named Fred Gallop. He was one of the first dozen or so engineers hired by Horst two decades ago when they set up shop in a small hangar over at Mojave Airport. Very smart guy, at least technically, and extremely hard working but an absolute weenie when it comes to confronting folk who aren't measuring up, especially if those poor performers happen to be engineers. He also doesn't know crap about marketing to the government although he sure as hell thinks he does.

"You'll also meet the VP of our Engineering team, a kraut named Siegfried Schmitt. Goes by 'Siggy.' Siggy is very solid technically but doesn't give a damn about cost or schedule commitments and he thinks our government customers are technically stupid which, as you know, is a very dangerous and corrosive attitude. Again, he was one of the engineers hired in part of the original Dirty Dozen and is quite a trip. Fred loves the guy so it's a first among equals situation relative to the other VPs. Fred has an office just down the hall and Siggy is holed up with his engineers in a large building toward the other end of the runway. Both of them and 'Rock' will join us for lunch with Horst once the demonstration is over and the VIP is on her way back over to Edwards AFB."

There was a knock on the door and Sugar cracked it open and announced softly, "Sir, Rock is here. Are you ready for him?"

"Yes, send him in!" Hopalong bellowed.

Drones

CHAPTER FOUR

Sugar opened the door as Orville stood and a rather large and thickset man, bent forward a little at the waist, lumbered into the office clutching a small black zippered item in his left hand. With no gray in his short-cropped brown hair, he looked younger than Orville expected but the oddly stiff and plodding gait made him, at the same time, seem much older.

Hopalong, seated with his back to the door, pushed the chair to his right back from the table and simply said, "Rock, this is Orville. Orville, Rock. Here Rock, have a seat."

"Pleasure to meet you!" Orville beamed with a bright smile as he stood and extended his right hand.

Rock just nodded slightly, mumbled something Orville could not understand and shook his hand very briefly. Orville was surprised by what could only be described as a very feeble handshake and by the almost complete lack of eye contact. Wow, this dude has no social skills at all. That must be what Hopalong meant by "a bit of a fucking pill," Orville concluded.

As Rock and Orville took their seats, Hopalong continued, "Gents, I've got to attend a meeting next door with the Customer Relations team honchoing this morning's VIP visit. Need to make sure this damn dog and pony show for Horst and our VIP guest comes off without a hitch. Shouldn't take more than about 30 minutes. You two can just stay here until then and use my office to get acquainted."

As he stood to leave, he looked at Orville and smiled. "Orville, I still remember the visit by those industry VIPs you pulled off back at Lakenheath. You did a great job," he said. "Boy, those were the days," he added with a sigh as he patted Orville on the shoulder and left the room.

After the door closed, there was an extended and awkward silence as Rock drummed the fingers of his left hand on what Orville now guessed was a black leather notebook or journal of some kind that Rock had placed on the table. Without looking at Orville, with his eyes focused downward on the black notebook, Rock finally cleared his throat and began.

"Well then, I guess it's good to have you here. Usually, I hire all the program managers. At the very least, I get to interview the candidates and make my personal recommendation so this is very unusual. First time actually…." Rock's voice trailed off into a mumble that Orville couldn't quite hear.

Orville didn't quite know how to respond. He was surprised, and a little pissed actually, that anyone would start off a relationship on such a sour note. However, he had worked for many different people during his years in the Air Force and at General Atomics and although some of his bosses had challenging personalities he had always found a way to make it work. This was just going to be another "learning experience" but he was confident he would again find a way.

"Well, sir, obviously I don't know anything about your normal staffing process so I accept your assessment that my hiring was out of the ordinary," Orville offered and then added, "I do think I have the abilities and experience to succeed here."

"Yes, yes," Rock interrupted in a slightly condescending tone, his eyes still downcast. "I have read your resume. You have a good enough background I guess but I have a question for you. Why did you leave General Atomics?"

Orville noticed that when he asked the question Rock had stopped the finger drumbeat and had lifted his eyes from the little book. He was now staring directly at Orville.   Orville stared back and replied evenly, "Well, I had a very messy divorce and felt I needed a little change of venue."

"And that's it?" Rock asked as he raised an eyebrow, still staring at Orville.

"Yes, that's IT!"   Orville was getting more pissed since Rock's tone and expression strongly suggested he thought there might be more to his GA departure, maybe even some job performance issues. As Orville glared back, Rock returned his gaze to the little black book on the table and continued.

"Well, I just don't understand why the General went outside the normal process and then assigned a 'green bean' like yourself, no offence, to such a critically important program. I like to have my new program managers get to know our culture and procedures here first and come up to speed slowly over a few years on smaller, less vital efforts. Only after they have proven themselves to me, based on their performance and their fit within our culture, do I assign them to bigger, more critical programs. It just doesn't make sense to me. It's all happening too quickly.

"Anyway, I've asked my deputy, Larry Power, to find a Director-level office for you somewhere in this building. He'll arrange some admin support for you too. I've also assigned a deputy to support you. He's a young guy but he's been here a little while and knows all the players and how we operate. His name is Joel, Joel Lackman.

"I've been running the program with a little help from Joel up until now and I'll need to stay very much involved until you are fully up to speed. There's a dedicated program area in Hangar 5. Has a SCIF and everything. You'll have a small office there too. We plan to brief you in on the program basics and some of the technology involved later today, but only at the Secret level. It'll take a while for the customer to do their security investigations and clear you for Top Secret. You'll need to take a polygraph too, which will take some time to schedule. Like I said, I'll need to be heavily involved for a while. Do you have any questions?"

Rock looked up briefly as he asked the question but when Orville replied "No, sir," Rock's eyes went right back to the damn black notebook.

"Your resume tells me you have done a lot of operations and test management but that's not quite the same as being accountable for meeting all the cost, schedule and technical baselines of a major defense contract. You'll need to spend some time with Power. He can fill you in on our operating culture and who the key players are and also recommend some online training you should take. The key for PMs here, and I tell this to all my PMs, is that you need to *be on it*. The support from other departments is probably not as strong as you're used to enjoying. Some of our processes are perhaps a little weak too. We've come a long way very quickly, from a very small company providing quick reaction capabilities to operators with critical and urgent needs to a mid-sized company that needs to perform on normal government contracts and we're not quite there yet which is why I say our PMs really need to *be on it*. PMs here at Acme need to follow-up and then follow-up again and not assume something is going to happen just because it should.

"You're also going to have to deal with an absolutely terrible customer. Your government counterpart has been the Program Director for over 4 years now and things have just got worse and worse. I really don't understand why but he's become more and more contractual and legalistic and is just downright adversarial now. He's the worst I've ever dealt with, a first class asshole. Our performance ratings have really deteriorated lately and those poor scores will make it harder to win future business so we need to turn these ratings around. I figured he would be gone a year or two ago but he's still there.

"Last bit of advice is to watch your engineers. Engineering is a super strong discipline here at Acme. They're used to calling the shots. Don't surrender to them and outsource your engineering judgment or they will make program decisions for you that will give you cost and schedule headaches. Come and see me if this is happening and I'll talk to the Engineering VP. The important thing to remember is that no matter why things got messed up in the first place, Fred Gallop will hold me and the PM accountable regardless."

Orville was about to ask Rock a number of questions about the customer relationship and the engineering versus PM authority issues when the door swung open and Hopalong barreled in and declared, "Orville, Luscious is waiting for you. Rock and I will see you at lunch."

As Orville and Rock stood, Hopalong added, "Rock, hang around a minute. I've got some go-do's for you that surfaced at the meeting I just had." Rock nodded and Orville said, "See you both at lunch then," as he grabbed his parka and walked out of the office.

Drones

CHAPTER FIVE

"Better put that parka on," Luscious cautioned with a wink. "We have a short drive in my turbo cart." Luscious drove Orville to a trailer where he met with Security, completed a few short questionnaires and had his photo taken. He left with a picture badge whose yellow border denoted he was a regular Acme employee. Subcontractors and part-time consultants had their own colors. Orville's badge also had a small "S" in the bottom right corner that indicated he held a Secret clearance.

Back in the golf cart, Luscious announced, "And now, we're off to Hanger 51. You'll meet your new deputy, 'Malibu,' and get in-briefed on your program."

"I thought his name was Joel something?" Orville inquired.

"Oh yes, Joel Lackman, but the General gave him his nickname when he learned Joel had grown up somewhere near Malibu and had been an avid surfer. He's a good guy. Has his head screwed on straight. You'll like him."

"And 'Hangar 51?'" Orville laughed. "You've got to be kidding me."

Luscious grinned and emitted an enchanting little giggle. "No, I'm not. Siggy gave it that label. Siggy Schmidt is the Chief Engineer here. It's officially just Hangar 5. I guess we do have a lot of second names and aliases around here. Must be the isolation," she concluded.

As Luscious parked the cart in a spot that read EXECUTIVE on the curb, she told him that tomorrow he could just swipe his badge on the readers at the two perimeter gates and then park his vehicle here. At the door, she suggested he try his new badge. He did and heard the locked door to "Hangar 51" click open.

Orville followed Luscious into a small lobby. Straight ahead, an extremely large, whiskered, armed guard hovered impassively over a counter. To his right, he noticed someone stand and walk toward him, right hand extended.

"Good morning and welcome. I'm Joel Lackman," he said. Lackman was tall, tanned, blue-eyed and youthful looking with his hair coiffed in the latest style. Yes, Orville thought, he could certainly see this gent as a surfer dude.

"Thanks Joel, I'm Sam. Sam Wright. But I think I'm going to be stuck with being called Orville here at Red Rock," Orville replied.

"I understand. Well, if you're willing to be Orville, I guess I can accept Malibu," he answered with a big grin before turning to Luscious and adding, "Good morning, Luscious, and may I say you look particularly awesome this morning."

Luscious blushed ever so slightly, smiled and replied, "Why yes, you may say that, and thank you, Malibu."

Orville felt a slight churn in his stomach and instantly felt jealous of the relationship, if any, that existed between Luscious and Malibu. The feeling didn't make any sense. He had no proprietary claim to Ms. Lopes. Hell, he had just met her, but he sincerely wished he had been the one to tell her she looked "awesome." She certainly did.

Luscious recovered her composure quickly and continued, "Orville, Malibu will have you for a few hours. I'll return and pick you up when it's time for lunch." With that, Luscious turned and walked out the door. All three men watched in silence until there was nothing left to admire. "Looks great, coming or going," Malibu solemnly intoned and Orville agreed. Even the hulking guard nodded his assent. Orville wondered if women like Luscious had any idea about the true extent of their power over men.

Pointing toward a sign-in roster on the counter, Malibu directed, "Just go ahead and sign your name on the last entry. 'Gabby' here filled in everything and I've already signed as your escort. We'll get you Hangar 51 access today and tomorrow there will be no need to sign in or be escorted. Right now, you and I need to place all our electronic devices in a locked container. It's over there," he said pointing to an array of keyed lock boxes next to the door on the left. "No recording devices at all so you'll have to lock up that fancy toy on your wrist too."

Orville signed in as 'Gabby' watched mutely. After he and Malibu locked up all the restricted equipment, Malibu swiped a card that was attached to his badge holder and put his hand flat against a palm reader to the right of the door. After a few seconds, the thick door slid open and the two men walked into a long, brightly lit and empty corridor with about a half-dozen closed doors on either side. As they walked down the empty corridor the door slid closed behind them and Malibu started to talk.

"Each door leads to a SCIF which we built to protect the sensitive compartmented information associated with certain programs. Each SCIF has a number of STU phones that allow you to have secure, encrypted communications. Outside this facility, there's not a whole lot we can discuss.

Ultimately, you'll need access to about half these programs but today you'll be exposed to just two. After your security in-brief, I'll give you a quick dump on those two programs at the Secret level."

Malibu stopped near the end of the corridor and faced an unmarked door to the right. He punched in a numeric code, turned a large handle and pushed open a massive metal door. It was like going into a safe at Fort Knox, Orville thought. The door opened into a surprisingly large enclosure. As Orville looked around, Malibu shut the door and rotated a handle to lock it.

Orville saw offices along walls to both the left and right. In the middle was a maze of cubicles and there was a mezzanine level above with additional offices. The place hummed with energy as youngish men and women, all rather casually attired, hurried about. Malibu acknowledged a few greetings and then shepherded Orville into the first office along the wall to the right. As he pushed open the door, he announced, "This will be your Hangar 51 office. Mine is right next door."

Orville walked past Malibu and into a small, sparsely decorated office. The furniture was all metal and looked like government surplus. Seated at a small circular conference table was a short, older man, a little past stocky. Without standing or shaking hands, he simply introduced himself as "Stumpy Lyons" and asked Orville to take a seat.

Malibu closed the door and stood while Stumpy in-briefed Orville to two Special Access Programs, Daedalus and Ares. Stumpy gave him a magnetic-striped swipe card for each program and took a palm scan of his right hand. Stumpy also provided a 6-digit code for each program he told Orville he needed to memorize. He told Orville that he had been hired as the Ares PM and that the Daedalus PM was someone named Demosthenes Dukakis. Stumpy told him that a number of folk on the Ares team were cross-briefed on Daedalus too and that the program colors on the special access badge holders would let him confirm the person he was speaking to enjoyed appropriate program access.

Finally, Orville was told that he was only being cleared today to Ares Level II but that a PAR request had been submitted to the government customer requesting access to Level IV based on his new leadership position. As Orville signed two in-brief forms, Stumpy asked if Orville had any questions. Orville had many questions but decided to save them for Malibu so he just said, "No questions and thanks Stumpy." His main concern at the moment was remembering the two 6-digit codes especially since they seemed to share a lot of the same numbers.

Stumpy stood and said, "Tomorrow, your cards, the palm reader and the individual numeric codes will all be activated and you'll be able to enter this hangar and the program area on your own."

As soon as Stumpy left, Malibu told Orville he needed something to drink so they walked to a small canteen a few doors away. The coffee was free and Orville filled up a small Acme Aviation mug that Malibu retrieved from a cabinet above the Keurig. Malibu grabbed a Mountain Dew from the refrigerator before they walked back to Orville's office, closed the door and sat at the small table.

Malibu was obviously ready to deliver the big "dump" he had promised but before he could start Orville asked him to describe his background and experience. Malibu began by talking about his first job at Northrop in the Los Angeles Airport area following graduation from Cal Poly but Orville interrupted, "No, please go back to the beginning. Where were you born? Where did you grow up?"

Orville learned that Malibu had been born in Chicago to Jewish parents and had moved to Calabasas, an affluent town in the hills just west of the San Fernando Valley, when he was about 3 years old. In spite of the early departure from the Windy City, Malibu declared he was a long-suffering fan of the Chicago Cubs. His father was an aerospace engineer who had made his way up the ranks and retired as a Northrop mid-level executive. His parents had divorced when Malibu was in elementary school. Malibu and his older sister were raised by their mother who remained in the Calabasas area.

Under a joint custody arrangement, he and his sister spent alternate weekends with their father whose major contribution to Joel's upbringing was teaching him to surf at Malibu, just a short drive over the coastal mountains on Las Virgines Road. Joel attended Calabasas High School where he lettered in soccer as a central defender and in track where he ran the half-mile. He also surfed a great deal, often getting up very early and driving to the beach for 30 minutes of pure joy before school. "I was the only Jewish surfer dude in my school," he proudly asserted. Malibu went to Cal Poly and graduated with a degree in Aerospace Engineering. Then, with some help from his father, he went to work immediately after graduation at a Northrop facility near LAX.

In response to a question from Orville, Malibu explained that he had left Northrop after 15 years because he wanted to escape the bureaucracy of a large, many-layered aerospace business and work for a smaller, more streamlined and agile company. His father knew some senior engineers working at

Acme and an interview was arranged. Although Malibu had a strong background in the preliminary design of RPAs, he had really enjoyed the challenges of managing a design team, meeting cost and schedule requirements and interacting with customers. The Acme engineering managers were disappointed he didn't want to work in the Design Department but sent him over to meet with Larry Power in Programs, an organization that had just been stood up.

"I guess 'Idle' was impressed," Malibu concluded. "He made me a job offer on the spot. I was employee number 295 and the first PM they hired that had industry program management experience from somewhere other than Acme. Everyone else they called a PM at the time was pretty much a homegrown Acme engineer who had simply been assigned to worry about the things management has to worry about. It won't take you long to figure out that engineers pretty much run Acme and program managers are just here to do the stuff that engineers simply don't want to do. Of course, and I don't want to come across as too cynical, but PMs are also the first to be blamed if those engineering decisions don't quite work out." Malibu's face lit up in a big grin as he delivered this assessment.

"Yes, Mr. Bottom warned me earlier not to let Engineering call the shots and said that I should let him know if that happens so he can talk to his counterpart," Orville said.

"Well, good luck with that," Malibu replied with a loud laugh. "Siggy is his counterpart and he just rolls over poor old Rock. Fred and Siggy are very, very close and are not about to let any PM assert too much authority over Engineering. So tell me about yourself."

Orville didn't reply immediately. He was still thinking about what Malibu had said about the weakness of program management at Acme and what it was going to take to overcome this cultural obstacle and succeed.

"So you were 15 years at Northrop and how long have you been here?" Orville asked after a long pause.

"My 10th anniversary here at Acme will be this September," Malibu replied. Orville just nodded but he was shocked to learn that Malibu was actually a 25-year aerospace veteran and had to be in his late 40's. He had guessed Malibu was at least a decade younger. Somehow his face had not been worn down by all the sun, wind and dry heat of the Mojave.

Orville then recited his own biography. He was born in a small town in central Kentucky, the oldest of four children, three boys and a girl. He was raised in a very Catholic Irish-English family and attended the University of Kentucky in nearby Lexington where he received a B.S. in Mechanical Engineering. He had lettered in basketball in high school. "No surfing nearby," he added with a smile. Inspired by an uncle on his mother's side who had been an Air Force test pilot, Orville had joined Air Force ROTC in college. Orville then quickly summarized his Air Force flying assignments, his experience at General Atomics, and even described his recent divorce as the catalyst for leaving General Atomics. He also disclosed how his long-standing relationship with Boyd had led him to Acme.

When Orville finished, Malibu asked him about his brothers and sister. Orville replied that one brother was in the oil business in Houston and the other was an attorney in Dallas. His sister, the youngest in the family, had become a nun.

"A nun?" Malibu exclaimed with a smile. "You said your family was 'very Catholic' but when you described your divorce I figured maybe not so much. I didn't know women even became nuns nowadays."

Orville laughed. "Well, for one, I'm not a very good Catholic in spite of my upbringing. I guess the term is 'lapsed.' But my little sister was another story. She was a very pretty and very talented girl. It was quite a shock to me actually. I was stationed in England when it happened and I couldn't believe it. My mom was very happy though. One of her ancestors had been in the same order long ago and Caroline took her name when she entered. Unfortunately, my sister passed away a few years ago. Breast cancer. She wasn't even 40 years old." Malibu was stunned by this unexpected disclosure and didn't know what to say. To escape the awkward silence, Orville grinned, raised his right hand and initiated a mock benediction as he added, "So, anyway, if you ever need to be blessed, Malibu."

Malibu quickly raised his hands in mock protest and said, "No, no blessing please. I might melt! Orville, I'm really sorry to hear about your sister."

"Thanks," Orville replied. "My mother and brothers were there when she passed. She was very serene and ready. Now, tell me what you can about Acme and these two programs."

CHAPTER SIX

Malibu briefly outlined the history of RPAs: how a quarter century earlier, General Atomics had captured the market for unmanned Intelligence Surveillance and Reconnaissance platforms with their Predator series aircraft and had later weaponized these aircraft. From Malibu's perspective, this success resulted from a combination of strategic vision, persistence and some very good luck with regard to the timing of an urgent customer need. These inexpensive aircraft were designed to operate in war zones. With the imperative of keeping the system costs low and affordable, a fairly high level of attrition was acceptable; after all, no aircrew lives were at risk and there wasn't too much concern about where they might crash in an overseas combat zone.

Later, RPAs were required to operate in national commercial airspace, or at least transit this airspace while they climbed to and descended from cruise altitude. This resulted in a dramatic increase in the standards of flight certification. As a result, RPAs now had to be much, much safer, almost approaching the safety and reliability requirements of manned systems. Those new requirements had significantly eroded the initial cost advantages of these increasingly expensive systems and encouraged the major aerospace companies to undertake efforts to erode General Atomics' early market dominance. Malibu then expressed his admiration for GA's ability to withstand this intense competition and the many rumored efforts by major aerospace companies to buy the company. He characterized their current production version, Pred F, as the very best value product available in the medium-altitude, long-endurance market niche.

Of course, Orville was very familiar with this summary. He had been the Test Director for both the Pred E and Pred F series aircraft. He knew that Pred F, as good as it was, offered only marginal value above new competing designs from Lockheed, Boeing and Northrop and that GA's cash cow in recent years had been the sale of earlier models, especially Pred D's, to trusted foreign partners while also selling non-weaponized, ISR-only versions to other nations approved by the US government. Of course, there was a very good long-term business supporting these large operational fleets worldwide, addressing their obsolescence problems and upgrading their capabilities either in the field or back in southern California.

Malibu then described how Acme had recognized GA's strong market position and had decided from the outset to focus on RPAs that could operate in more hostile, non-permissive environments, in airspace protected by the sophisticated and highly integrated air defense systems of a technologically savvy potential enemy. As a result, from their early days in the hangar at Mojave Airport, Acme had invested in technologies that would enable a RPA, operating on Day One of hostilities, to degrade and ultimately destroy the air defenses of a sophisticated near-peer enemy, quickly achieving a level of air dominance sufficient to allow manned aircraft to roam the enemy's skies at an acceptable risk. As Malibu put it, GA had focused on aircraft flying extreme endurance missions that would be too "dull" for a manned system while Acme had focused on unmanned aircraft that could fly missions that were too "dangerous" for a manned solution.

Malibu recounted how many years earlier, the Air Force had conducted a formal competition for a new long-range strike aircraft and that RPA designs, as well as manned designs, were initially considered as potential solutions. In the end, the Air Force couldn't quite get out of their manned aircraft comfort zone and purely unmanned solutions were disallowed. However, there was a requirement for an unmanned version of the manned solution in the future. Nonetheless, the initial fielding would be a manned "B-21" bomber offered by Northrop. Of course, Orville was well aware of this background since the "B-21" had just recently achieved a well-publicized first flight milestone.

Malibu then disclosed that unknown to all but those with the proper clearances and required access, the US government, intrigued by Acme's original purely unmanned offering, had eventually initiated a highly classified, unacknowledged special access program to mature a number of critical technologies required to eventually develop and produce an unmanned long-range power projection capability. These technology maturation contracts were awarded to Acme on a sole source basis, without a competition. A few years ago, the Air Force decided that all the key technologies had reached maturity levels that supported a new start to develop an unmanned bomber system. Again, a highly classified contract was awarded to Acme on a sole source basis. This revelation completely shocked Orville. He thought, at the least, he would have heard rumors of such an effort.

Malibu further explained that Acme's long-range strike solution was actually a number of unmanned systems. One was Daedalus, an ultra light, extremely long endurance vehicle that flew at altitudes above 100,000 feet and could stay aloft for many weeks, not just a few days, running on solar power as needed. Its proposed surveillance and reconnaissance payload had capabilities that allowed intelligence to be gathered in many cases without even the risk of overflight. This extremely persistent ISR development program was being managed by "Demos" Dukakis. Daedallus would securely link its vital intelligence to warfighters worldwide and, most importantly, link to the complementary Ares platform.

Ares was a long-range strike RPA that used a combination of speed and negligible radar and IR signatures to survive in a very sophisticated, hostile air defense environment. The big breakthrough had come from Siggy, whom Malibu labeled "an alchemist when it comes to exotic materials." Siggy had developed "magic coatings" that, along with advanced shaping and buried powerplants, had dramatically lowered both the radar and IR signatures ("our vehicles are flying ice cubes!") with only modest weight and drag count penalties.

After 50 years, "true multispectral stealth" was now achievable and affordable too. Malibu added that today's VIP guest, whom he referred to only as "Jane, " was there to witness a flight demonstration of a subscale Ares prototype. The test mission today involved flying multiple passes of the prototype on "our radar and IR signature ranges," to measure key parameters and provide signature plots of both against azimuth and elevation in near real time. Malibu said this same demonstration had occurred for some Air Force VIPs about 3 weeks ago but now the classified customer wanted to see for herself.

Malibu explained that Ares itself would be a large vehicle with a takeoff gross weight of about 250,000 pounds. It featured 2 enormous internal bays capable of carrying over 50,000 pounds of payload. Inside those huge bays, on universal racks, Ares was being designed to carry a mission-dependent mix of about 50 small RPAs, each weighing no more than 1,000 pounds. Some of these RPAs would be for self-defense, if needed, to supplement the Ares on board defensive laser. Other RPAs were being designed specifically for other missions such as attacking air defense radars or surface-to-air missile installations or airfields or even airborne fighter aircraft. Others would be dedicated to jamming or other forms of electronic attack. All of these small RPAS would be designed to be expendable and as inexpensive as possible with service lives measured in hours. And all of them would be designed to self-destroy in a kamikaze mode or self-detonate if needed to prevent any possible technology exploitation of a recovered, intact RPA.

Orville was truly amazed as he tried to comprehend the complexity of what he was being told. " This is all very interesting," he said. "A lot of people were wondering what Acme was up to. You'd enjoyed some success years ago competing with us, excuse me, with GA, in some niche markets with your early RPA products, especially the Excalibur. It just seemed like your basic design philosophy had traded away extreme endurance for speed, which only makes sense for certain missions and certainly not the very long endurance missions GA was focused on addressing. Now, this system of systems approach has decoupled the largely mutually exclusive requirements of high endurance and survivability by allowing two very different but complementary designs. It's amazing the government would fund such an expensive approach with dedicated platforms. Those idiots are usually trying to force a single platform solution to address multiple and often conflicting mission requirements."

"Well, we have some problems there," Malibu replied. "The Air Force Big Safari customer said they want us to develop these systems like we did many years ago, on an expedited, get-it-to-the field ASAP basis and not through the dot all your I's and cross all your T's bureaucracy of a normal SPO-run procurement. We bid these development contracts based on a number of stated and unstated get-it-to-the-field as soon as possible assumptions. Unfortunately, it seems the customer has been operating in a traditional acquisition environment for so long that they really can't stand letting us do things in the quick reaction way any longer. They appear to have selective amnesia and keep inserting additional steps and efforts we believed had been set aside. Certainly, these efforts were not priced in our bid. The government wants to have it both ways, cheap and comprehensive, and we simply can't do both. The customer is very frustrated with our cost and schedule overruns and lately they have even been waving the flag of a potential termination for performance. I'll come back to that a little later but first, let me explain another big challenge.

"We had partnered with Boeing on a purely unmanned long range strike solution and we had jointly advocated a collaborative effort on a Daedalus/Ares type technical approach before the Air Force decided not to allow such a such a strictly unmanned solution in their long range strike solicitation. After our quite successful technology maturation efforts, it was clear the customer wanted to continue with a classified follow-on full-scale development effort. However, they insisted that we carry Boeing as a teammate so they are now a subcontractor and we have a requirement from the government to give them at least a third of the total work content. They are developing a number of the small mission-specific RPAs that will be carried by Ares and also have some major structural elements of the Ares vehicle itself. Also, they are providing some key avionics and sensor systems on the Daedalus vehicle. Of course, they knew about the government mandate for their content and were stubborn as hell in negotiations regarding their work share. Not surprisingly, their costs are currently overrunning. They are actually absorbing over 40 percent of the budget, which is really squeezing the hell out of us as the prime.

"To be candid, we need their help in certain technical areas but they are a huge pain in the ass to deal with and a lot of our senior people don't trust them at all. In fact, some of them are convinced Boeing wants the program to perform poorly and be cancelled because Boeing believes this would allow them to lead a follow-on program with minimum Acme involvement. I'm not usually very paranoid but they may well be right. Of course, there's always the possibility that Boeing, with its deep pockets, could just buy us although the Schwarz brothers are very unlikely to sell.

"We are on a cost plus type development contract which includes building full-scale prototypes of both Daedalus and Ares and demonstrating some key performance parameters in a series of flight demonstrations. Potentially, Boeing could compete with us for the follow-on low rate initial production contract. Anyway, you can see the problems all this causes with both parties holding their cards very close to the vest and avoiding the true collaboration that's needed for success."

"I do see. Malibu, I was also told we had a lousy customer Program Director. What's your take on him?" Orville asked.

"Colonel Brush is the name of your customer counterpart. His handle is 'Wire.' He's not great but we could do a lot worse, in my humble opinion. I have a constructive working relationship with him but Rock hates his guts and it seems 'Wire' hates him back. Our senior leaders all think he's a fool and Wire knows that's how they feel about him. As his nickname suggests, the Colonel is pretty brash and can sometimes be downright abrasive. Rock doesn't seem to be able to deal with that personality aspect either, especially it seems to me, because the Colonel is not a rated Air Force officer.

"On the plus side, Wire is very accessible. You can call him anytime, night or day, and he will take action. You might not like his actions but he isn't remote or passive. My main complaint about Wire is that he doesn't rein in his team, especially some of his over zealous engineers when they start interpreting ambiguous contract language in a way that drives a lot of unbid and unpriced content into our job jar. For too long, we have just accepted these changes and avoided getting legalistic with their contracting officials. I think we naively thought that as long as we did what they wanted technically they would accept the cost growth and schedule delays and take care of us in the end. In hindsight, that was a big mistake. Daedallus is only slightly overrun but Ares has submitted three cost overrun proposals in the last 30 months and the projected cost at completion is now about 30 percent above the originally negotiated cost. Not good at all.

"Poor Wire is getting hammered by Air Force senior leadership for overrunning the program's allocated schedule and budget baselines and he's hammering us in turn with marginal and unsatisfactory performance assessments. It flows downhill as you know. I expect he thought he would be promoted to general officer out of this assignment and now he sees our poor performance as having denied him this advancement. Wire's now seeking financial consideration from us for numerous missed deadlines and totally discounting the government's very real contributions to those delays.

"As you know, it's absolutely critical to ensure your customer is seen as successful in their world if you want a good relationship. Anyway, as soon as you're ready, maybe next week, we'll arrange a trip to Dayton and you can start the process of building a better relationship. Believe me, with Rock hopefully less involved now that you are here, there's nowhere to go but up at this point."

"Pretty unbelievable," Orville exclaimed. "But you are spot on. Rule One is to ensure your customer counterpart is recognized as a big success in their organization. And, if your customer is a fool, well you've just got to find a way somehow to suffer that fool, gladly or not. So what's the story with Rock? How did he let things get to this point?"

"Well, confidentially, Rock just doesn't seem to understand what you and I obviously agree on, which is a real mystery given his extensive background on the government side. Rock was the capture team leader for our part of the original long-range strike campaign, when we thought the RFP would allow purely unmanned offers. The later technology maturation contracts were pretty much run by Siggy in Engineering. However, once the customer decided to go forward with the two black programs, Rock was assigned as program manager for both Daedallus and Ares

"Shortly after that assignment, the overall Programs VP left unexpectedly. In my humble opinion, Fred just panicked and quickly promoted Rock to head the Programs organization. The organization announcement identified Demos as the new PM for the two programs. In reality, Rock never stopped running both of them. I guess he felt success was just too important to Acme and I'm sure he didn't trust Demos, or anyone else for that matter, to lead such key efforts. Demos told me that when he complained to Rock about this micro-management, Rock just told him that Fred expected him to be immersed in the nuts and bolts, to 'be on it' as he likes to say, so he felt he had no choice but to be heavily involved.

"About a year ago, Demos had suffered enough it seems and finally went direct to Fred. He explained to Fred that he had no real authority, that Rock was constantly contacting people on his team directly, asking questions, sometimes giving direction and often setting up meetings that Demos was not even invited to attend. Fortunately, his team would inform him of the meeting and he would typically just insert himself and show up. On one occasion, Demos had made a quick 3-day trip to meet with the customer back east. By his calculation, Rock conducted a dozen program-related meetings with his program team just in that brief interval.

"Even more frustrating for Demos was the fact that as the programs, especially Ares, fell behind schedule, Rock always seemed to forget about his intrusive decision-making. Demos felt he was going to be left holding the proverbial bag. Fully accountable but with no real authority. Demos asked Fred to assign him elsewhere and even hinted at leaving the company.

"Fred talked Demos into staying the course by taking the Ares program away from him, letting him focus on the better-performing Daedallus effort. He promised to talk with Rock about keeping his hands off Daedallus, although he acknowledged that Rock would likely be unable to follow this direction. That's a big problem with Fred. He doesn't like to be confrontational or to be seen as less than collegial and Rock knows he can get away with just selectively ignoring him. I get the impression the General would like the company to be run more like a team where you can be benched or even traded away if you don't perform. Fred has always treated the company more like his own large family and you can't fire a family member. Anyway, all Fred offered was a plan to give some additional responsibilities to Rock as a way to decrease the time Rock would have available to mess around with Daedallus. A pretty pathetic approach in my humble opinion. Unfortunately, Rock has a lot of energy and works very long days so there's almost no limit to the damage he can do.

"Fred also directed Rock to hire someone for the Ares PM job. I applied but Rock told me I was too inexperienced. I have more PM experience than he does so that was a big disappointment to me and, confidentially, I have been exploring options to leave the company ever since. Anyway, Rock's interviewed and rejected a number of outside candidates. I think there have been about a half dozen. A few of them were extremely strong candidates, probably too strong in fact. I'm pretty sure Rock saw them as a threat to his own VP position. He's an amazingly insecure guy and with good reason I might add since he's way over his head in an executive role. Finally, it seems the General had enough of this foot dragging and just hired you. I suspect Rock's not a happy camper."

"Sounds like Rock has a big problem with trusting others," Orville interjected. "And maybe there's a Peter Principle thing going on here too? He's finally been promoted to an executive-level position where he's incompetent, simply unable to take his hands off the flight controls and let someone else fly the airplane."

"Funny you should use that flying analogy," Malibu replied. "A while back, the two of us were on a King Air flight to visit a supplier in Arizona. Right after takeoff we had some kind of electrical problem and had to return back to Red Rock and land. The cockpit door was open and as Rock watched the crew handle the emergency he became more and more agitated. He even yelled at the flight crew when he became concerned about their handling of what seemed like a pretty routine emergency. It was all very distressing. Hell, he was a test pilot. I expected him to be calm and collected in a situation like that."

"Yep, as long as he's the one dealing with the emergency situation and flying the aircraft, he probably would've been calm and collected," Orville interrupted. "But the truth is that he's apparently very uncomfortable letting others manage a challenging program or fly an airplane during an emergency. He just doesn't trust other people enough. I can see I'm really going to have my hands full dealing with Rock while I try to build a better customer relationship and also improve our contract performance."

"Yes, you are," Malibu agreed with a smile.

"*WE* are, Malibu," Orville quickly corrected. "I am going to need your expertise and counsel in a big way. You know the company culture, the personalities as well as the programmatic issues. I really appreciate your candor in sharing all this with me and I promise to treat our conversations as confidential. I also promise always to be straight with you."

"Thanks, boss," Malibu replied. "By the way, after your lunch, I've scheduled an informal get-together with your Ares leadership team. Should be about a dozen folk. Of course, we can do this tomorrow if you'd prefer some time to prepare your comments or build some charts."

"No problem with today," Orville answered. "I'm as prepared as I'll ever be, but I do have a question. What can you tell me about Ms. Lopes?"

Malibu let loose a big laugh. "Well, finally down to some real business," he exclaimed. "I can tell you she's an awesomely good-looking woman. Do you need any more information?"

"Well, that doesn't tell me anything that isn't fucking obvious," Orville answered with a grin. "I was hoping you might know just a little more."

"Let's see," Malibu said, still laughing. "Like most of the other attractive single women here at Red Rock, I dated her for a few months shortly after she came to work here a few years ago. She was born in Brazil. Portuguese father and Japanese mother. She grew up there in a large Catholic family. Believe it or not, she actually went to a convent for a while but left the convent when her parents emigrated. Her father was an engineer with Embraer in Brazil and went to work for Boeing somewhere near LAX when they moved to the States. She ended up attending Occidental and got a degree in Business, then a MBA at UCLA. Went to work in Human Resources at a Catholic Hospital in Torrance as I recall, close to where her parents and a bunch of her siblings lived."

"Wow," Orville said. "You know a lot. So how did she end up at Red Rock?"

"Well, she got married while she was working at the hospital but it only lasted a few years. She didn't talk much about her marriage and I guess I wasn't that interested in her ex anyway. I know she was devastated by what she called her 'failure.' She decided she needed a big change. Her father had a friend who had come to work here at Acme and here she is."

"Thanks for all the data," Orville said. "So, if you don't mind, what happened between you and Luscious?" Orville found it interesting that both he and Luscious had fled to Red Rock after a divorce.

"Well, nothing happened, unfortunately," Malibu replied with a grin. "You know, I don't like to brag but I'm usually pretty successful with women I really go after and boy did I really go after her. Brains and beauty. I mean, here she was on the rebound from a failed relationship. It should've been so easy but I never even got close to first base.

"I've tried hard to understand why. For a while, I rationalized that it was a case of a devout Catholic girl who might be a little anti-semitic but I knew that's really just bull. Or maybe she had a bad attitude toward men in general at that time. Anyway, a number of guys have pursued her since with the same result as far as I know. She certainly dresses for attention and comes on a little flirty but in the end, it's seems like it's all show and no go."

"Well, thanks for all the info. If she's not in a relationship right now, I might just have a run at her myself. My ex is Korean and I might still have a touch of yellow fever when it comes to women."

"Well, good hunting then. I'm pretty sure she's not seeing anyone these days," Malibu said before being interrupted by a knock on the office door. A man Orville had not seen before pushed the door open slightly, peeked in and said "Luscious is on her way to pick up Mr. Wright for lunch." Two minutes later, Orville and Malibu met Luscious in the Hangar 51 lobby.

CHAPTER SEVEN

Luscious drove Orville back to Building 1 where he had met Hopalong earlier. As Luscious dropped him off, she advised, "Lunch is in the conference room to the right, just before you get to the General's office. Everyone's there already so just grab some food and go on in. I'll shuttle you back to Hangar 51 when lunch is over. Sugar will call me."

Orville thanked her and told her she didn't need to pick him up. She gave him a cute little pretend pout of disappointment but quickly agreed. Orville made his way to the General's office area. When he was just inside the outer door, he saw Sugar standing next to a buffet that had been set up outside the conference room.

"Hi, Mr. Wright," she beamed. "Just grab what you want and go on in. The others just went in with their food a minute ago. What would you like to drink?"

"I'll stick with coffee," he answered. "Black, of course. Thanks."

"Of course, black," Sugar replied with a conspiratorial smile. Orville grabbed a tuna wrap, some pasta salad, and a bag of potato chips. Sugar handed him his coffee in a disposable cup and Orville entered the conference room.

Seated at the far end of the large mahogany table, an older man stood immediately and walked quickly up to Orville before anyone else could move or say a word. Orville noted that his gait was smooth and purposeful. He was wearing a starched white shirt and a conservative crimson tie. Orville was barely able to place his coffee and food plate on the table before the man gripped his right hand in a vise-like handshake. "Welcome to Acme, Mr. Wright. I'm Horst Schwarz," the man intoned. "We're very glad to have you join us. Now, please take a seat and enjoy some lunch."

From his gait to his grip to the piercing blue-eyed gaze, the strong impression was one of supreme self-confidence, vitality and power. Here was someone used to being obeyed. He was of medium height with tanned, chiseled features that defied the loosening and sagging of flesh over time. Orville figured he must have had a facelift since he looked considerably younger than his 80 or so years. He certainly looked younger than Hopalong, seated to Horst's immediate right, who had to be a dozen or so years younger. There were quick greetings and introductions to the others at the table. The conversation over the next hour was largely focused on "Jane" and the just completed

VIP demonstration. Orville listened and studied his fellow diners.

Seated cross from Hopalong, on Horst's left, was Fred Gallop whose greeting has been warm and congenial. If Schwarz's manner had seemed like that of a bird of prey, Gallop's was more like that of a big, friendly ostrich. Fred was very tall, at least 6 and a half feet, with straight white hair and a bushy white moustache. He had a goofy lopsided grin and seemed a very genuine and amiable sort.

To Fred's left sat Siggy Schmitt. Siggy still had a slight German-sounding accent despite his many years living in the States. Maybe he thought it added value and didn't want to lose it, Orville mused. Siggy also had a moustache that added a little width to a long narrow face. He sported red suspenders and a matching red bow tie that clashed with a shiny bright orange shirt. His hair was dark, longish and seemed to be totally unacquainted with comb or brush. Across from Siggy sat Orville's new boss, Rock Bottom, who didn't bother to greet Orville or even acknowledge his arrival. Orville's clear impression was that Rock wasn't happy that Orville was there dining with the other VPs and Mr. Schwarz. Orville saw that Rock had brought his little black book to lunch and that he took notes periodically throughout the discussion. He also observed that Rock was left-handed.

Listening carefully, Orville concluded that the VIP demo had gone reasonably well. However, there had been some IR signature "anomalies" that needed to be addressed, both technically and politically. In the discussion, it was clear to Orville that only Fred and Siggy, and perhaps Rock to an extent, truly understood the technical issues. When Rock offered what seemed to Orville like a quite reasonable technical comment, Siggy immediately dismissed it. Orville judged that Siggy would have embraced the input if it came from anyone other than Rock and sensed throughout the meeting that there was a real tension in their relationship.

Horst seemed most upset with the quality and appearance of the paint that had been applied over Siggy's magic coatings and was also displeased by some "unacceptable untidiness" in a corner of the Ground Control Station where the VIP had witnessed the demonstration. Hopalong was focused on how the good but less-than-perfect results should be characterized in some program update briefings he was scheduled to deliver at the Pentagon at the end of the week.

When Siggy estimated it would take "at least a month" to evaluate fully the IR data and then define and validate a fix, Hopalong roared that engineering better go on high alert and "burn the midnight oil because 2 weeks is the most the

bubbas in DC will be able to stomach at this point."
When Siggy tried to push back, a red-faced
Hopalong slammed his large fist on the table and
yelled, "Two fucking weeks!" Everyone sat silent
for a few seconds after the outburst before Fred
calmly stated, "We'll have a good answer for you
in 2 weeks."

As Orville cleaned up the coffee that had spilled
out of the small opening in the lid of his cup with
Hopalong's fist blow, it was apparent to him that
they were all well accustomed to Hopalong's
volatility and frequent profanity. Interestingly, no
one else at the table used any colorful language
throughout the lunch, only the General.

A few minutes later, the meeting ended and
Orville found Malibu waiting just outside the
conference room. Together, under bright, cloudless
skies, they walked back to Hangar 51 as Malibu
pointed out a number of site facilities and briefly
outlined their purpose: the software integration
laboratory, the systems engineering building, the
supplier management team building, the
composites shop, the final assembly and checkout
building. To Orville's surprise, he also pointed out
a small recreation center with two lighted tennis
courts.

Malibu asked Orville about his impressions of senior leadership and, as he had promised, Orville was candid and unguarded as he passed along his initial observations and absorbed Malibu's replies.

"Yes, Horst can come across as bit cold. He has a reputation as a real hard-nosed businessman and someone who is tough as nails in negotiations and I believe it. One of his favorite sayings is, 'Always buy straw hats in December' and he's continuously looking to acquire undervalued assets. It seems to me he's usually right in his valuations, and timing too. Anyway, I'm told his brother Hannes was always the easier one to approach but he's been MIA for the last few years with health issues," Malibu offered in response.

"What about Fred Gallop?" Orville inquired. "He seemed like a friendly guy and very smart technically. What's his background?"

"Advanced degree in mathematics, as I recall," Malibu answered. "He was the original software coding guru. Unfortunately, he still treats the software folk like prima donnas who can do no wrong. To be candid, their processes and metrics are not as robust as they need to be. I understand Fred's very religious too. Doesn't drink alcohol or swear."

"He must be in a state of constant irritation when Hopalong is around," Orville said, laughing.

"Well, you'd be surprised. Fred doesn't seem to mind at all that the General cusses like a sailor. They always seem very deferential to each other when I've been present but I'm told they go at it sometimes, usually over how to best go about marketing some product or capability to the government. The General's convinced he knows best how to get things done with the government customer and based on his track record since coming to work at Acme, I'd say he's mostly right," Malibu explained.

"My only concern with the General is that his early success here was based in good part on promising and then delivering new capabilities to the field very, very quickly. It required Herculean efforts by a small, very skilled and very dedicated team. It also required a customer who didn't insist that everything had to be perfect. Better was the enemy of good enough. Unfortunately, today's customer expects perfect, but still insists on yesterday's very compressed timelines. I worry, based on these new realities, that we are over-promising," Malibu added.

"Yes, I saw some of that schedule pressure at lunch," Orville said and briefly described the

General's fist-pounding moment. "What about Siggy?"

"Well, all you need to know is that Siggy is that he's the guardian of engineering preeminence at Acme," Malibu continued. "And, by the way, he and Fred are good friends and avid tennis players. I think they had the recreation center built just so they could justify some tennis courts. When they're not on travel, they usually play doubles there on Tuesday and Thursday evenings. If you play tennis and don't have a life away from Red Rock, it's a good way to kiss their butts."

"Well, unfortunately, I don't play tennis," Orville said, laughing. They entered Hangar 51 and proceeded to Orville's new office in the SCIF. Malibu told Orville he had 40 minutes to prepare for a meeting with his direct reports and offered to help prepare any charts he might want to use for what Malibu labeled a "Hello Briefing." Orville said thanks but that he would just talk with the team.

The meeting took place in a small conference room just beyond the canteen. In addition to Malibu, 10 people attended, all male. There were a few team leads, a chief engineer and the functional leads for contracts, procurement, manufacturing and logistics support. With one exception, they all seemed younger than Orville. The one exception was James Papadopoulos, the manufacturing lead, who mercifully went by the label "J.P." and seemed to be about 60 years old.

Orville outlined his expectations and the program operating culture he wanted to establish for the Ares Program, one that was open, transparent, with no secrets and no shooting of messengers. He explained that he fully intended to trust people to run their program teams without a lot of interference and that he would be tolerant of the occasional honest mistake as long as the same mistake was not repeated.

This was the way Orville had always operated, both in the Air Force and at General Atomics, and he believed there was really no other way to run a squadron or a program efficiently and effectively.

The team was very attentive and engaged throughout. Several of the team leads pointed out that PMs at Acme were not truly empowered and that this was a problem. All the functional leads, including the chief engineer, agreed with this perspective. Orville said he completely understood but nonetheless intended to operate differently on the Ares program. He expressed confidence that the company would necessarily transform itself over time. He sensed acceptance of his operating rules but also a great deal of skepticism that they could successfully create such a sub-culture within Acme.

That evening, on the drive home to Victorville, Orville's head spun with all that he had absorbed during his first day at Acme. He was simultaneously worried and exhilarated by the host of problems and the challenges they represented.

\

CHAPTER EIGHT

The first two months at Acme passed quickly as Orville settled into his new job. As expected, Rock continued to micromanage the Ares Program, scheduling multiple daily meetings to address the crises of the day in addition to the several regular weekly reviews that were part of the operating rhythm. Superimposed on all these meetings with Rock were pop-up technical deep dives and periodic programmatic reviews with Fred. Somehow, only Hopalong seemed to be able to operate without this constant blizzard of up-channel story telling.

In Orville's view, all this reporting and the work required to build charts and brief them was absorbing far too much of his team's valuable time, leaving far too few minutes available each day for actually working program problems and staying close to the customer. Orville started to maintain a record of all this story telling and asked his direct reports to do the same.

Orville also maintained a log of all the occasions where Rock skipped over him completely and communicated directly to members of the Ares team. Orville told the team that they should be fully responsive to Rock's questions and requests for meetings but to include Orville on any electronic responses and to invite Orville to any meetings Rock asked to be scheduled. Rock rarely called Orville directly. Of course, this hierarchy jumping had happened everywhere Orville had worked before but nothing on the scale he was recording in his log. Orville realized it was going to be even harder than he anticipated to break this habit and insert himself into the communications and management loop.

A constraint on this intrusive habit should have been the security reality of the program. Orville was becoming increasingly concerned that sensitive topics were being discussed with Rock on non-secure lines and in Rock's Building 1 office, which was not cleared for top-secret classified discussions. Rock's willingness to "talk around" these very sensitive and classified issues made Orville very uncomfortable.

During his second week at Acme, Orville and Malibu traveled to Wright-Patterson AFB in Dayton Ohio to meet the Air Force Program Director, Col. "Wire" Brush. The Colonel was a short, sturdily built officer with something of a Napoleonic complex. He lived on the ragged edge between being completely over-bearing and merely abrasive but Orville had dealt with more difficult personalities in the past. Discussing "Wire" with Malibu over drinks at a bar in Fairborn that evening, Orville conceded that although the Colonel was, "the cockiest SOB I ever met who wasn't a fighter pilot," at least he seemed smart and knowledgeable. They both laughed and agreed he wasn't the monster-run-amok described by Rock and Fred and that they could do business with him. In any case, there was really no other choice.

Over those early months, Orville came to appreciate Malibu's value not only to the Ares Program but also to the enterprise at large. Simply stated, Malibu thought like a program manager, and possessed what seemed like an innate ability to keep the cost, schedule and technical performance baselines always in fine balance. Technically, he could more than keep up with the engineers but his knowledge of contracts and other business aspects was also exceptional. Clearly, Malibu should have been promoted to Director long ago. Although Orville was grateful for his own opportunity at Acme, he also realized that Malibu would have been a perfectly good choice to lead the Ares Program.

Because he had worked for 15 years at Northrop before coming to Acme, Malibu had a perspective that those whose industry management experience was confined to Acme did not enjoy. Importantly, he understood the Acme culture and the quirky personalities of its many self-described "mavericks." It was a culture that seemed to prize getting things done quickly in an *ad hoc*, improvised, almost process-free manner. Most of the senior employees typically abhorred any detailed planning or analysis and thrived on extinguishing the many "fires" that this approach necessarily caused. Anything that smelled of process rigor was labeled "Big Company Bull Shit" or simply "B.C.B.S." and immediately rejected.

Shortly after his trip back to Dayton, he ran into Luscious in the Building 1 hallway. Impulsively, and rather awkwardly, he asked her if she'd like to go out to dinner sometime. His invitation had come like a bolt out of the blue and she wore a seriously puzzled look as she paused to consider his proposal. As he waited, Orville realized he had no idea where she lived. Maybe, like many others working at Red Rock, she lived north of the site, towards Ridgecrest or some other inconvenient place. After what seemed a long silence, he was about to apologize for his rash invitation when Luscious smiled and sweetly replied, "Yes, I'd love to." Orville felt his pulse quicken and his knees wobble slightly as they worked out the details of a pickup at her place at 7PM that Saturday. He was relieved to find out she lived in Victorville too, no more than 3 miles from his own apartment.

Over the next 2 months, they were together a half dozen times. They discovered they both enjoyed horseback riding and Orville took her to the glider port at Tehachapi where he introduced her to the majestic views of the Sierras from a sailplane. She introduced Orville to tennis and although he wasn't very good, especially in the high winds of a Mojave spring, he did enjoy watching what Luscious could do to a tennis skirt. Orville found her to be bright, charming and utterly seductive. On their 5th "date," she even kissed him, on his cheek. It was the most arousing kiss he had ever experienced.

In his 3rd month at Acme, the frustrations of working for Rock finally exceeded Orville's threshold for action. Throughout his career, the people he worked for had always appreciated private candor, no matter how prickly they might be if someone pushed back, however politely, in public. As a result, he scheduled a "private" meeting with Rock with the vague subject: "Management Issues."

Since Orville told Rock's admin this was a one-on-one session, he was unpleasantly surprised to find Larry "Idle" Power seated at the small conference table in Rock's office. Rock explained that he had asked Idle to sit in since he was "sort of my deputy" and "works a lot of our management issues."

Orville began by sharing his specific assessments of the major Ares Program issues, all of which he characterized as surmountable based on the top-level corrective actions he outlined for each issue. He then went on to express serious concern about "a culture of arrogance" at Acme in which its employees constantly ridiculed both the customer and key suppliers for "just not getting it" and seemed completely unwilling to seriously consider the perspectives of other non-Acme members of the larger Team. Rock and Idle listened without comment.

Within the company, Orville described the engineering function in much the same way, arrogantly holding itself as the fountain of all knowledge and never being held to account when their decisions, either technical or programmatic, were in error. Orville added that at some point in the past it almost seemed to him that Acme engineering had simply invented the Programs organization just to do the stuff they didn't want to waste their time doing and, of course, ultimately to be blamed for any failures. In this instance, both Rock and Idle agreed wholeheartedly. However, when Orville asked what the company intended to do to fix this, neither one offered any good answers.

Rock suggested that we needed better, more assertive PMs who were willing to push back and not "out-source" their judgment to the engineers. He wondered out loud whether we were hiring the wrong people or not training them adequately or both. Orville interrupted to suggest that it wasn't the quality of the PMs but an operating culture in which PMs were held fully accountable but had no commensurate authority while Engineering on the other hand exercised considerable authority but was never held accountable.

Rock suddenly changed the subject and went back to Orville's earlier observations about customer and supplier relationships. He flatly denied Acme had any relationship issues with major "subcontractors," although he added that Boeing was a "total pain in the ass" on the Ares effort. When Orville said that he thought Colonel Brush was far from the worst government manager he had encountered, Rock angrily declared, "Well, regardless, he's a total asshole."

After an awkward pause, Orville moved on to describe his perspective that senior Acme leadership didn't seem to trust the Acme team, including people at the Director level, to make decisions and run their programs. Rock quickly became very defensive and said that this wasn't true at all and insisted "Acme people were empowered." It was clear to Orville that this micromanagement critique was an old and open wound for his boss.

After Rock emphatically denied it was an issue, he reversed course and explained that Fred was the reason he had to be so heavily involved since "he is always asking me detailed questions and expects me to know all the specifics." He then went on to explain that in Orville's case, he was simply too new to the company and to Ares to run the Program by himself. When Orville said he disagreed and asserted that after 3 months he now was ready to proceed "without training wheels," Rock forcefully and bluntly said he disagreed completely and rather bluntly reminded Orville who was the boss.

Orville had made his points and should have just let the meeting end on this professional disagreement, calmly stated. Instead, he went back to Rock's excuse that Fred was the reason he had to be so engaged in the details. Orville politely suggested that Rock should be willing on occasion just to tell Fred he didn't know the answer to his question but would provide a full answer to him ASAP. That was apparently too much candor for

Rock who exploded, "That's just not the way things work around here!" With that forceful declaration, Rock pushed back from the table, stood up and walked back to his desk. The meeting was over.

As Orville left, Idle pulled him into his office, which was just across the hall from Rock's. Idle was a balding man with a florid complexion and an earnest manner. He had been hired as a production planner in the early days but was not a member of the Dirty Dozen. Idle did not have a technical degree and that had certainly limited his advancement in such a technically oriented company. In Idle's office, with the door closed, Idle confided to Orville that he agreed with almost everything Orville had said and offered to work with him as a "fellow change agent." He said he knew how things worked at Acme and together they could help transform the company "without ruffling too many feathers." Orville appreciated Idle's offer but doubted that any real change could occur at Acme without some major "feather ruffling." He thanked Idle and left. In the months that followed, Orville came to realize that Idle was all hat and no cattle, a cautious man with a perfect nickname.

Two days later, Orville was unexpectedly invited to a "private" meeting with Fred. Fred greeted him warmly and explained that Rock had told him that Orville had a number of concerns and that he'd like to hear about them directly from Orville and not secondhand from Rock. Fred asked if Orville had shared his concerns with the General and Orville assured him that he had not. Fred seemed relieved.

Orville then summarized his observations to Fred who listened attentively. Fred agreed there was far too much complaining about the customer and that we needed to get past personalities and recognize what we share in common. He expressed the hope that Orville would be able to make a fresh start with Wire in this regard although, "Colonel Brush is a very difficult person to work with." He also acknowledged that we were far too willing to throw our industry partners under the bus when it was our job as the overall system integrator to deliver on the contract. "We own it as the prime," he concluded. "In the end, it's an Acme product in the marketplace."

However, Fred disagreed that Engineering was too powerful. Even after Orville provided some recent examples of "engineering overreach," Fred dismissed these instances as "anomalies" and said he believed this wasn't a real issue in such a technology-based enterprise.

On the micromanagement issue, Orville told Fred that over 70% of his time was devoted to meetings with either Rock or Fred, leaving about 20% for working with the customer and a paltry 10% for actually leading the Ares program. Orville expressed the conviction that what he labeled "internal up-channel story-telling" should be no more than 25%. Fred was shocked by these numbers and suggested that most of the 75% must be due to Rock. Orville provided him with data that showed that all of Fred's weekly written status reports on on-going technical issues, in addition to a host of established bi-weekly, monthly, bi-monthly, quarterly and tri-annual meetings accounted for about half of the 75%.

Fred said he would revisit his operating rhythm and see what could be done to lessen the burden. He also said that he knew Rock would never change his micro-managing *modus operandi* but promised that he would give Rock some additional responsibilities in other areas that should dilute the amount of attention Rock could devote to Ares. Orville was very disappointed in these vague commitments as well as Fred's indirect approach to dealing with Rock. Why couldn't Fred just tell Rock to stand down and let Orville run Ares, he wondered? It felt like superficial collegiality run amok.

Finally, Orville told Fred he thought Fred himself was too involved in "tactical decisions" that should be made at much lower levels in the company. Fred asked for an example and Orville described a recent incident where Fred had done some "managing by walking around" and dropped in at the office of the Flight Test Director on a Friday afternoon. They had discussed a test planned for Saturday morning and Fred learned that the Test Team planned to use a Revision G Software Load. Fred felt that it would be better to use an earlier version, Revision F, instead. As a result, the Test Plan, which had already been reviewed and approved by the government customer's Technical Review Board, had to be revised and presented again for their review and approval. The test planned for Saturday was delayed until the following Tuesday and schedule margin had been unnecessarily eroded.

Fred just shook his head. He acknowledged that he knew intellectually that he should avoid getting involved in specifics like what Software Revision should be used for a particular test. However, he explained that changing this behavior would be very hard in practice since "I have been making all the important calls since the early days at Mojave Airport." Orville pointed out that the company was now far too big for this centralized approach, that Acme was failing to develop leaders who were comfortable with "making the tough calls" and then being held accountable for their decisions. Fred then confessed that in this specific case he was really just expressing his opinion regarding which software version should be used and did not know it had been taken as direction. "I guess I have to quit thinking out loud too," he said reflectively.

The meeting ended abruptly when Fred's admin knocked on the door and announced, "Siggy and a large group of engineers are here for the 10 o'clock meeting." She also told him he had to take a call from Horst first. Fred hurriedly thanked Orville for his observations and said they should revisit them periodically. As Orville left the office and closed the door, he noticed the familiar faces of some engineers who worked for him on Ares. He asked one of them about the topic of the meeting with Fred and was told it had to do with potential technical solutions to the flutter issue.

Orville was very familiar with the flutter issue and had worked it hard within his Ares team over the past few months. He had briefed Rock a few times on alternate technical approaches and indicated a preferred solution. Rock had concurred and the team had been working the implementation of needed design changes with their government counterparts back east.

Orville approached Siggy and said he'd like to sit in on the meeting. Siggy, a little embarrassed, told him it wouldn't be appropriate since this was an "engineering only" meeting. Orville insisted that the program office should be represented. Siggy emphatically said no. Orville, furious at this exclusion, managed to control his anger and left without another word.

Outside the building, he immediately phoned the Ares Chief Engineer who he noticed was not there with Siggy. Jim was not aware of the meeting with Fred. Jim informed Orville he knew there were some engineers in Flight Technologies who didn't agree with the Ares team's technical solution and speculated they might be trying "an end run" to Fred. Orville told Jim to go to Fred's office ASAP and get into the "engineering only" discussion.

Even more upset now, Orville went directly to Rock's office and told him what was happening. Rock just shook his head and promised he would talk to Siggy about it that evening. The next morning, Rock called Orville and said he had talked with Siggy about the incident and that Siggy was unapologetic. Later Rock discussed this with Fred and he had just shrugged his shoulders and grinned. A few days later, Orville learned that his team had been directed to work a new technical approach to the flutter issue, one that "Siggy and Fred approved." It was not the one that his team had been advocating with the government and now everyone had to switch gears. Wire had called Orville and he was understandably not a happy camper. The unwillingness of some to accept the team's consensus decision and their readiness to take their appeal in secret to a higher authority was deeply troubling. Even worse from Orville's perspective were the cost and schedule penalties associated with implementing the newly directed change.

Orville became more and more frustrated with the Acme operating culture as the summer progressed. He realized he had made a big mistake and should have done some due diligence on Acme before just jumping on Hopalong's invitation. The only positive thing in his life at the moment was Luscious.

Orville and Luscious were seeing each other quite a bit now and although he knew he was totally smitten, he was not sure she felt the same way about him. In some ways, that made her even more captivating. When he described her to one of his old colleagues at General Atomics, a former fighter pilot and Thunderbird solo, as a woman he would like to marry, his friend had roared with laughter. "You've got to be fucking kidding me,

Orville!" he exclaimed. "You just got divorced. Think of it this way. It's like you just landed after an intense air-to-air combat engagement where your bird took some cannon rounds and you've got a major sucking chest wound. Instead of going to the hospital for surgery and many months of recovery, you tell the medics just to stitch you back together while you remain in the cockpit and the ground crew reloads your guns and refuels your bird. Then, you takeoff and re-engage with the enemy. You've just gotta be shitting me, Orville. Marriage? You're not ready to get back in that damn fight. You need a few years to recover, boy!" They both laughed hard at the tortured analogy. By late summer, Luscious had even kissed him softly on the lips. This was a damn slow courtship, he thought, but she was certainly worth the wait.

CHAPTER NINE

Orville and Luscious enjoyed a great Labor Day weekend with some old friends of hers at Lake Havasu on the Colorado River. Afterward, things between them seemed to change abruptly. For the very first time, Luscious turned down a dinner invitation; then, a week later, another rejection. More followed. She would explain she was either too busy or just too tired. When they talked on the phone, she seemed distracted and in a hurry to finish the call. Throughout, Luscious insisted nothing was wrong while Orville kept replaying that weekend at Lake Havasu over and over in his head, trying to uncover clues that would help him solve the mystery of her now distant behavior.

At work, Orville was becoming more and more frustrated. He had been at Acme for over 6 months and Rock was essentially still running the Ares program. Orville had no belief that this would change anytime soon and although Fred had seemed sympathetic, he remained unwilling to deal directly with Rock on the issue. If Fred had assigned additional responsibilities to Rock as promised, these new duties had absolutely no effect on Rock's frequent intrusions into the active management of the Ares program.

Orville had shared these frustrations with Malibu who jokingly suggested, "Maybe Rock has pictures of Fred in some compromising situation?" They had both laughed. Malibu was also very frustrated. He had worked at Acme for 10 years and should have been a Director long ago. Watching how Rock treated Orville, he came to realize that even if he was promoted to Director and assigned to lead a major program, the problem of Rock and the dysfunctions of Acme's small company micromanagement culture would remain. He shared with Orville that he was looking for a job elsewhere, including a position with General Atomics in the San Diego area. Orville offered to help with the GA job pursuit if needed. He also told Malibu he had decided to go around both Rock and Fred and share his frustrations directly with the General. Malibu promised he wouldn't commit to work elsewhere before the end of the year.

During his months at Acme, Orville had only seen the General about a dozen times and always in large forums. Hopalong spent 2 to 3 weeks each month on the road trying to position Acme for new business. He also had to invest a great deal of energy back east just to keep contracted programs like Daedallus and Acme "sold" in the face of continuing performance hiccups and what everyone at Acme believed were Boeing efforts to undermine the current programs.

Although Hopalong had encouraged him on his first day at Acme to come see him if Rock was a problem, Orville had been reluctant to take advantage of this invitation. It just wasn't his style to operate outside the "chain of command." Even his private meeting with Fred had been at Fred's invitation. Now however, he felt he had endured enough. In fact, Orville now planned to leave Acme the following spring, on the 1st anniversary of his employment there. He was delaying his resignation only to avoid a contractual obligation to pay back a small signing bonus if he quit before 12 months had elapsed. Orville just hoped he could last another 6 months. When he contacted Sugar to schedule a meeting, she said the only time free on Hopalong's calendar was at 6:30PM, late that Friday.

Sugar was gone and the outer office empty when Orville arrived at 6:25PM. He walked up to Hopalong's office. The door was slightly ajar and he was about to knock when he heard a soft invitation, "Come on in Orville and have a seat on the couch." Orville was surprised by the muted sound of a voice that seemed far removed from the loud, boisterous welcome he expected.

Orville entered, closed the door and moved toward the sofa in the conversation area. As the General approached, he noticed that Hopalong had dark circles around his eyes and moved very slowly. He conveyed an overall impression of deep fatigue. As Hopalong settled deeply into one of the overstuffed chairs facing the sofa, he sighed, offered a slight smile and said, "It's good to see you, my friend. Hope you're doing all right. Well, what's on your mind?"

Orville thanked Hopalong for staying late to meet with him on a Friday evening. Hopalong surprised Orville by telling him he had one more meeting at 8:00PM. Good grief, Orville thought, no wonder the General looks beaten down if he's working those kinds of hours.

Orville began his recital of the problems he had encountered working with Rock and how he felt he was a non-value-added but still accountable layer between Rock and the Ares team. He said he had talked about this to Rock on numerous occasions and had even met once with Fred. As he described his frustrations, Hopalong would offer a weary nod now and then while his large frame seemed to be slowly disappearing into the overstuffed chair.

Suddenly, out of the blue, Hopalong interrupted, "Orville, would you like a drink? I could sure as hell could use one."

"Yes sir"

"Follow me, then," Hopalong commanded as he stood and made his way toward a wooden cabinet directly behind his desk. Orville followed in close trail. Hopalong spun the cabinet on some hidden axis and depressed a button somewhere on its back. He slid open a panel that revealed two wooden shelves stocked with a few tumblers and an assortment of hard liquor bottles. "What's your pleasure?" Hopalong asked. "Got some scotch, some bourbon and a little tequila too. But no water or ice."

"I'll have a bourbon."

"Maker's Mark OK?"

"Absolutely. It's almost homegrown."

"Ha! That's right. I almost forgot you're a damn briar. Well, I'll have one with you." The General seemed to be regaining some vitality with just the prospect of a drink. Hopalong poured generously into two tumblers, offered one to Orville and proposed a toast "to the great Commonwealth of Kentucky."

As they clinked their tumblers, Hopalong asked, "It is a fucking commonwealth, isn't it?" Orville grinned and nodded.

After they walked back to the conversation area, Hopalong said, "I fully understand the micromanagement issues with Rock and the ball is now in my court. But I need to share something else with you."

They settled into their chairs. Hopalong paused, took a sip of bourbon and continued, "This is absolutely fucking confidential. Even beyond Top Secret. Got it?" Hopalong paused again and stared intently at Orville.

"I understand, sir," Orville said.

"Well, to get directly to the point, our boss Horst has been kidnapped. He just fucking disappeared into thin air during a trip to your commonwealth about two weeks ago," Hopalong started.

"What was he doing in Kentucky?" a shocked Orville asked.

"There's some kind of annual horse show in Lexington and he hasn't missed attending this September goat rope for at least the last decade. Usually buys a pony or two," Hopalong answered.

"Must be the yearling sales at Keeneland," Orville mused out loud.

"Yeah, yeah, that sounds right. Now, just be quiet and let me talk. So Horst flew into the Lexington airport on the company's Lear and stayed with a prominent family who own a couple hundred-acre horse farm not far from this Keeneland place. He's known this family for many years and has stayed with them a few times in the past.

"On his second evening there, he attended a little soiree at this Keeneland place. He hired a local limousine service to take him there since he knew he would be drinking a little and didn't want to be driving his rental car with a buzz. Again, Horst apparently had used this same Lexington limo service year after year for these kinds of social events during the horse sale. Like most of us, he is a creature of habit and in retrospect that might have made him an easy target.

"Anyway, several witnesses confirm he left the shindig just after midnight. No one saw him actually get into the limousine but a guard at the gate did see the limo leave and logged it out. When his hosts checked the guesthouse after he didn't show up for breakfast the next morning, there was no Horst and no evidence that he had ever returned to the farm following the soiree. No evidence of forced entry or anything else suspicious either. The driver and the limousine itself are also missing."

"Good grief," Orville exclaimed. "You said this all took place 2 weeks ago. Have we heard from the kidnappers? Do we have any leads? What are the police doing?"

"Yes, the FBI is deeply involved," Hopalong continued. "Right now, they seem focused on the limousine driver and his history. Seems he might have had some interesting international travel over the years. He's only worked for the limo service for a year. Even though he was a junior driver, it was pretty easy to get assigned to drive Horst to the party since he is notoriously stingy when it comes to tipping." Hopalong took a long deep sip of bourbon and Orville noticed he had almost emptied it already. Orville's tumbler was still almost full so he took a big gulp.

"As for a ransom note, we heard nothing for well over a week but a few days ago a letter addressed to his brother Hannes finally arrived here at Red Rock. The letter is just fucking bizarre. It's very polite, formal sounding even, like something straight out of the 19th century. There's no demand for money either. What they insist on is that Acme exit the drone business as soon as practical. And, get this, they also insist we destroy all our relevant intellectual property. And there's no "or else" threat to Horst either. No deadlines. In fact, the letter says he's being comfortably detained and, if we failed to meet their demands, he will simply remain in their custody until he dies of natural causes.

"Interesting, huh? And listen to this. There was probably an attempt to kidnap the General Atomics chairman on the very same day. He had received an award, given a little speech at the Air Force Academy and was returning to Denver on I-25 at night. Some people in a dark gray pickup truck wearing ski masks pulled up next to him, pointed a pistol at him and tried to force him off the road. He said they nudged him a few times and there's evidence of those collisions on his rental car. He said they didn't shoot and didn't seem willing to really ram him hard. He told the authorities they eventually exited the freeway at someplace called Castle Rock after the two of them overtook some other cars also headed north on the freeway.

"The Chairman had called 911 from his car and the police were in Castle Rock looking for the truck about 10 minutes after the call but no joy. He told the police that once he figured out they were unwilling to hurt him, he just flipped them the bird every time they bumped into him. I don't know him well but I guess he's one tough sonofabitch.

Anyway, thank God he didn't get nabbed too. I need another drink."

Orville was trying to absorb all this. He had met the Chairman a only a few times during his years at GA. Thank goodness the kidnapping attempt had failed, he thought.

Hopalong stood, went to the cabinet, poured himself another drink and brought the bottle of Maker's Mark back with him. "Would you like a little top off?" Hopalong asked.

"Sure, thanks," Orville replied, lifting his tumbler. "So you said earlier the main thing the FBI is working on is the background of the limo driver?"

"Well, they are also analyzing the non-ransom ransom note. It was postmarked in Louisville and it seems that it was typed on an old 1970's vintage typewriter. It all seems so damn amateurish. We asked the FBI if our classified customer friends could help but were told that would be illegal without some foreign connection and that link had yet to be established. You see, the limo driver, who's an African-American by the way, converted to Islam about a decade ago and some of the international travel included a few jihadi hot spots.

So maybe a connection will be established that will allow the Agency to be brought in?"

"What else do we know about the limo driver?" Orville asked. "Was he religious before he converted to Islam?"

"Apparently, a quite devout Catholic," Hopalong answered.

"Wonder how that transformation happened?" Orville mused. "I don't think there's much of a Muslin population around Lexington."

"Well, you'd be surprised. Muslims keep a pretty low profile these days. You probably don't know there's a mosque in Victorville, even a small one in Ridgecrest. In fact, there's actually a good-sized mosque in Lexington. It's been there quite a while and used to have a pretty radical imam preaching there from what I've been told. Anyway, the FBI is looking into all that history.

"Let's see, what else do we know about this dude? For one, he isn't originally from Lexington. Abdul something or other grew up in a little podunk town about an hour west."

"Do you know where exactly? I grew up in a small town about 50 miles or so west of Lexington, a place named Cedar Springs," Orville blurted out.

"Well, I'll be damned! I think that's where the limo driver is from, Cedar Springs. I'm pretty sure that was it. Fucking amazing! Old Abdul spent some time in the Marines right after high school. Was married briefly, had a few kids, but got divorced and has lived pretty much by himself for the last 20 or so years. I've got some notes in my desk. Let me get them."

While Hopalong retrieved an unmarked manila folder from a locked desk drawer, Orville tried to process the strange connection between the kidnapping and his hometown of Cedar Springs.

"My God, that's my hometown!" he exclaimed after Hopalong sat down, pulled some sheets from the folder and confirmed the name of the town.

"I know, it's fucking weird," Hopalong agreed. "Let's see, here it is. He goes by Abdul Ali Khan. Spent a lot of years in Lexington but he lives now in an apartment on North Woodlawn Street in Cedar Springs."

"Do you know his birth name, before he converted?" Orville asked.

Hopalong studied his scribbled notes, then flipped the sheet over and after a few seconds said, "Here it is. Funny name for a Catholic boy but I guess a famous civil rights leader's name trumps everything else. Martin Luther Sims," Hopalong answered with a chuckle.

"Marty Sims!" Orville shouted. "I went to high school with a Marty Sims. We were teammates on the basketball team." They both sat quietly for about 10 seconds. Hopalong took a big swig of bourbon and looked directly at Orville.

"Well, Orville, you've got a new assignment," Hopalong directed. "We'll hand the Ares baton over to Malibu and Rock. You're on the damn CAT now."

"What's a CAT?" Orville asked.

"It's the Crisis Action Team that's working the kidnapping," Hopalong answered. "Next meeting is 7AM in my conference room on Monday. Now, help me clean up and hide the bourbon before my next meeting."

Hopalong's glass was empty but Orville still had two fingers of Maker's Mark in his tumbler. He downed it in one swallow.

CHAPTER TEN

It was a difficult weekend for Orville. In spite of his frustrations with Acme in general and with Rock in particular, he wasn't happy to give Rock this opportunity to even further assert his control over the Ares Program. He thought about calling Hopalong and asking if he could be a CAT member without abandoning his program leadership role but decided to wait until after Monday morning's CAT meeting before deciding whether to play that card.

He called Malibu on Saturday morning and told him that he expected an announcement on Monday that he was temporarily assigned to a confidential special project. It was awkward not to be able to specify just how long Malibu would be the acting PM. He explained to Malibu that he just wanted to give him a little bit of a heads up since, if it happened, he and Rock would have to decide how to communicate this change to Col Brush as well as to the Acme Program Team.

When Orville called Luscious on Saturday afternoon, he just got an answering machine. Afterward, he thought that his voice message must have sounded pretty pathetic. When she failed to return his call, he imagined she was with another man and that vision truly depressed him.

Orville thought a lot that weekend about his old high school basketball teammate, Marty Sims, and wondered if he really could have been involved in the kidnapping. Maybe, like Horst, he was just a victim who was being held captive somewhere along with Mr. Schwarz. He had met Marty a few times during his college days when Marty was visiting his mother on leave from the Marine Corps. Orville recalled the last time they met was long ago at a 10-year high school reunion in Cedar Springs. Marty was by himself and explained that he and his wife were in the process of a divorce. Marty had told him that returning to civilian life after years in the USMC and multiple combat tours had proven to be a difficult adjustment for him and that he didn't blame his wife at all for leaving him. After a restless, unsettled weekend, Orville was actually looking forward to the CAT meeting on Monday morning.

When Orville walked into Hopalong's conference room a few minutes before 7:00AM, he was shocked to see Luscious seated there. She was equally surprised to see Orville. Orville said a quick hello to her and then awkwardly introduced himself to two people he didn't recognize: a large African-American man with an Acme badge who introduced himself as a the Deputy Director of Acme Security and a tall, lean middle-aged man with a crew cut and a visitor's badge who simply said he was the "FBI case officer." Orville was so preoccupied with wondering why Luscious was there that he forgot their names immediately.

He was about to take a seat when another stranger walked in, with Hopalong in close trail. Hopalong introduced the stranger to Orville as Hannes Schwarz, Horst's son, who was named after his uncle. Hopalong explained that the young Hannes had flown in from Scottsdale, Arizona that morning. Hannes was considerably taller than his father but Orville noticed the strong resemblance immediately, especially around the eyes. He had heard of the younger Hannes but only knew he ran other companies that were part of the family's larger global business empire.

Hopalong introduced the other two men, Mr. Felt of the FBI and "Tiny" Robertson from Acme Security. He also introduced Ms. Lopes as the HR member of the CAT and someone who provided all the required administrative support. Hopalong explained to the attendees that he had invited Orville because of his quite amazing connection to the limousine driver, Mr. Sims. Orville was surprised that no one asked Hopalong how he came to discover that relationship given the secrecy surrounding the kidnapping. With introductions done, Mr. Felt opened a binder and briefed them on the latest status of the FBI investigation.

Mr. Felt's update focused on Mr. Sims' travel to Pakistan about 18 months earlier. Sims' mother said he had gone to visit a friend named Nawaz Suhrawardy and had been gone for about a month. Sims' mother had further explained that Mr. Suhrawardy had stayed with the Sims family during her son's senior year at Cedar Springs High School and that they had stayed in touch over the years. At this point, Orville spoke up and confirmed that he remembered a short, skinny Pakistani kid staying with Marty and attending their high school for a year. Orville described him as smart and funny with an impeccable British accent. Orville stated that Nawaz had several tall blonde girlfriends during his one year in Cedar Springs, liked to dance and party and opined that it seemed very unlikely he had now become a terrorist recruiter. Mr. Felt put on a professional sour face when he listened to Orville's amateur deduction. Orville also recalled that Nawaz's grandfather had been President of Pakistan at one time.

Mr. Felt was clearly irritated throughout Orville's interjection and interrupted him to state that the grandfather had been "Prime Minister, not President," of Pakistan in the 1950's.

Felt also confirmed that the CIA had now been brought in because of the possible foreign

114

connection to the kidnapping and they were working hard to identify where Sims had traveled in Pakistan outside the two weeks he had spent in Karachi with Mr. Suharwardy, whom the CIA described as a very successful businessman and not a particularly devout Muslim. Felt added that Mr. Sims had also visited Lourdes, France and Medjugorje in Bosnia about 10 years prior.

Felt briefed that a few years after Mr. Sims left the Marine Corps and moved to Lexington he started attending a mosque there and had formally converted to Islam about 8 years ago. At one time, the imam who preached there was considered somewhat extreme and the mosque had received a great deal of surveillance. He added that several members of the congregation were in fact FBI agents.

Although that imam was deported at about the time Mr. Sims began visiting the mosque, there was "some evidence" that Sims had associated with a few of the "less moderate" Muslims who remained. Mr. Felt said this "promising" part of the background investigation was also ongoing and might well establish some important links to Sims' travel since some of his mosque associates were born in Pakistan.

When Felt told them FBI analysts were still studying the letter, which he added was absolutely clean of any prints or DNA evidence, Orville asked if there was a copy of the letter he could read. Felt frowned but quickly handed him a copy of the short note while he continued with his update. Orville hunched over the one-page, single-spaced typed note and began to read.

To Orville, the note was truly amazing. It had a formal, polite and oddly philosophical tone and contained none of the jihadi rhetoric he expected from an author he assumed was yet another radical Islamist terrorist kidnapper with apocalyptic visions of the end times. Instead, the letter very calmly conveyed the author's sincere feeling of intense suffering for the sins of the world, with American drone use clearly considered as one of the world's major sins.

However, what really struck Orville was the repeated use of the phrase "Justice and Peace." Orville, and Marty too, had attended Catholic elementary and middle schools taught by the Sisters of the Most Holy Cross, an order of nuns with a Motherhouse not too far from Cedar Springs. This was the order that his little sister belonged to before her tragic early death. Phrases like "Justice and Peace" and "Unity of Love" and "Trust and Fellowship" were themes repeated over and over again by these sisters in a seemingly unending chorus. These other phrases were not in the letter but there were three repetitions of "Justice and Peace" in the short one-page note.

Orville's quick analysis was interrupted by Hopalong's announcement that the meeting was over, with the next CAT meeting scheduled for the same time on Friday morning. Hopalong thanked Mr. Felt for the update and asked that the Acme folk stay behind for a short follow-on meeting. Mr. Felt stood, offered some awkward farewells and exited, escorted by Sugar.

As soon as the door was shut, Hannes Schwarz forcefully announced that he had no trust at all in the US government and certainly not in the FBI whom he described as "a nest of bumbling incompetents." He said that anyone in the Bureau who was even "semi-competent" was now involved in the on-going investigation of the recent attack by radical Islamic terrorists on the Vice President and Secretary of State during their "secret" meeting at the recently opened Embassy of Kurdistan in Washington, D.C. this past July. Three Secret Service agents had been killed along with several Kurdish diplomats during an intense 5-minute firefight that left 6 terrorists dead. One of the attackers was captured. Another had escaped but had so far eluded capture in spite of a massive on-going manhunt.

Hannes opined that there had to be a senior level mole within the Administration for the terrorists to have known so much about the meeting's high-ranking attendees, its timing and location. As a result, Hannes told them he was conducting his own investigation, using a private security group in whom he had great confidence. He added he had no intention to share their conclusions with Mr. Felt or anyone else from the government.

Hannes briefed that "his guys" had already concluded that Nawaz Suhrawardy was certainly not a radical Muslim and had never been affiliated with any such fanatics. They also reported there was no indication at present that Mr. Sims had met any terrorists in Pakistan during his visit there although they still needed to run down a few leads in the Rawalpindi area before absolutely ruling out such contacts. Hannes added that, "I wonder how long it will take the feds to get this far in their investigation. My father will probably be long dead."

At this point, Hopalong said, "Of course, Mr. Sims may have been radicalized at the mosque in

Lexington or might even have self-radicalized on the internet."

"I'm not so sure this is a matter of Islamic terrorism at all," Orville suddenly blurted out. "I've been reading this letter from the kidnappers and there are some phrases in it that suggest to me at least the possibility that some Roman Catholic nuns might be involved."

"Fucking nuns? Really?" Hopalong almost shouted. "You've got to be shitting me, Orville!"

"Wait a minute, General," Hannes cautioned. "My guys are looking at the letter too and it certainly doesn't seem to have been written by some Koran-inspired nutcase. They have been looking at any number of groups that have been part of anti-war and anti-drone protests over the years and some of those participants have been from religious groups. Let's hear what Mr. Wright has to say."

With that invitation, Orville explained his family's long association with the Sisters of the Most Holy Cross whose Motherhouse was located about 10 miles outside of his hometown, Cedar Springs. He described their long-standing commitment to "Justice and Peace," the phrase repeated several times in the letter. He added that the nuns had also been active anti-war protesters over the years, not just marching and holding signs outside defense company facilities but also disrupting the shareholder meetings of some major defense companies.

"Sounds like a long shot, but someone has my father and we need to cover all the possibilities," Hannes asserted. "Any ideas as to how we should proceed?"

"Let me go to their Motherhouse and check it out," Orville offered. "They're always conducting retreats there. I'll just sign up for one and do some snooping around."

"Sounds like a plan to me," Hannes concluded. "I'll have one of my guys contact you and work with you on a detailed approach. If you do find something there, we need to make sure the cavalry is nearby. We don't need you to be kidnapped too, or worse."

With that caution, the meeting abruptly ended. As Orville and Luscious were about to leave the building, he grabbed her elbow and whispered that he'd like to have dinner with her at 7:00PM that evening. She looked at him and softly whispered, "Certainly." Orville was surprised to notice that her eyes were moist.

CHAPTER ELEVEN

Orville had a very nice dinner with Luscious. They didn't talk much about the CAT meeting other than recognizing that her heavy involvement on that Team and nothing he had said or done over the Labor Day weekend was the reason she had been unavailable and tired over the past several weeks. He was relieved. Another man was not in the picture. But when he dropped her off at her apartment she suddenly started to cry. She had made the retreat and travel reservations and knew he was leaving early the next morning for Kentucky.

Orville was surprised by this emotional display and how concerned she seemed about his personal safety. He tried to assure Luscious he didn't consider what he was doing as particularly dangerous. He told her that she shouldn't worry since he wasn't "the hero type" and was just going to look around.

Even though he had suggested a possible connection to the sisters, the more he thought about it, the more difficulty he had seeing these nuns commit such a serious and criminal act. He just didn't think it was all that probable that the God-fearing women who had taught him as a boy were kidnappers. Even if they were, he was just there on a retreat and certainly didn't intend to put himself in harm's way. He reminded Luscious he would be flying back to California next Sunday and they agreed to meet for dinner that evening.

Nothing he said seemed to reduce her anxiety. Finally she gave him a long wordless embrace, kissed him and quickly closed the door behind her. He could hear her sobbing on as he walked away. Again, he was puzzled by her reaction, which seemed a little dramatic, but he was also flattered that she seemed to care so much about his safety. Maybe there was a future here?

He left his apartment for LAX before 3:00AM the next morning and caught a 6:30AM flight to Chicago with a connection on to Louisville. He rented a car and drove about an hour to the small town of Shakespeare, Kentucky. As instructed, he checked into the Lafayette Tavern in the center of town where a room had been reserved in his name. Orville was very familiar with the Tavern. His parents had even hosted a small party there to celebrate his graduation from UK.

When he opened the door to Room #1, the Lincoln Suite, he was shocked to see a large man already seated in an antique chair by the window. The man stood up and walked toward Orville, extended his meaty right hand, and simply said, "Mr. Wright, I'm Bruno," as they shook hands.

"Please just call me Orville," Sam replied as he put down his carry-on bag. Bruno had called Orville on Monday afternoon and explained that Hannes had asked him to call. Bruno had told him that someone at Acme had booked Mr. Wright a room at the Lafayette Tavern in Shakespeare for Tuesday night and that he would connect with him there. Then, quite abruptly, Bruno had hung up.

Bruno looked to be a little over 6 feet tall and was built like a NFL fullback. In fact, he looked fit enough to suit up and play right now. Only the gray around the temples of his closely cropped hair and a deeply lined face suggested he might be too old to block a pro linebacker. He moved slowly and deliberately and conveyed a sense of immense, barely restrained physical power and menace.

Over the next hour, seated on a very hard antique sofa, that "must be stuffed with fucking horse hair" according to Bruno, they pored over an expanded satellite map of the retreat facilities and Motherhouse that Bruno spread out on a small table in front of the sofa. Bruno pointed out a few structures, large cabins really, in the woods near a private lake to the north of the Motherhouse that he said might be good sites for holding someone captive. The structures of interest were highlighted in red circles. He suggested Orville could take some exercise between retreat events and scout those sites. Bruno doubted anyone would be held hostage in the 2 dozen or so buildings that comprised the heart of the physical plant. Bruno also pointed out the fields of a working farm, barns, convent, dining hall, residence halls, infirmary, several chapels, the founder's historic cabin as well as the retreat center itself and the small apartment complex called Peace Haven where Orville would be staying. Way too much activity in these areas to serve as a safe keep for a hostage, Bruno observed.

He then gave Orville a special phone that had a voice encryption capability that would allow them to communicate directly without fear of electronic eavesdropping. The phone only allowed him to contact Bruno. And just in case he couldn't make a call, Bruno gave him a very special ballpoint pen. "When you push it to write, it alerts me that something has gone really wrong and you need immediate help. It transmits its position to me and can't be shut off once activated. My team will be staying at the Hampton Inn on the bypass around Cedar Springs and I will be wherever this fucking pen is with reinforcements in no more than 20 minutes. So don't use this damn pen unless you are in immediate danger." he warned. "We don't want to ride into town with pistols drawn and scare the little sisters just because you had a brain fart and used this pen to sign an autograph or something."

"Thanks 'Q'," Orville had said as a joke but Bruno didn't even smile. Instead, he snarled, "You're no fucking James Bond with a license to kill but if you're not careful, someone with such a license might just mort you out." Orville's smile quickly disappeared.

Bruno then asked if Orville wanted to wear a shoulder holster and carry a .45 caliber pistol. Orville declined. With that, Bruno abruptly stood up and walked to the door. As he opened the door, he looked back at the still seated Orville and quietly said, "I don't think you're going to find a damn thing there but be careful. Good luck." With that, he was gone.

Orville went downstairs and enjoyed a dinner of cornmeal-breaded catfish and a California chardonnay before returning to his room. He was asleep 5 minutes after he undressed.

After a shower and late breakfast on Wednesday, Orville checked out of the Tavern and headed out of town. He turned right at the golf course and drove past the Bluegrass Parkway, eventually passing the Marker's Mark bourbon distillery before turning again. This was certainly beautiful, green, rolling countryside he thought as he drove on. He took his time and even stopped once to soak in the view since check-in at the retreat wasn't until noon. After about 45 minutes, he was there. He parked and walked around the grounds for about 15 minutes. At precisely noon, he walked to the Peace Haven lobby area and checked in.

CHAPTER TWELVE

There were about a dozen people at the mid-week retreat and he met them all at dinner. Nice folk all, mostly from Kentucky and Indiana but a few from further away. There was a nice couple from somewhere called Clayton, just west of downtown St Louis and an older single woman from West Virginia. Orville was the only single man and the only person from further west than St Louis. An elderly priest, Father Cecil, had greeted them at dinner. He said some words about injustice and oppression throughout the world but quickly gave way to a Sister Susan Spalding who told them that their goal at Peace Haven was to provide a "reflective space" that would allow a brief escape from their busy lives. She said there would be an emphasis on solitude and silence, even at the three meals provided daily. If you really wanted to talk to others while there on the retreat, you could sign up for a partner (she held up a clipboard) with whom you could converse on any number of secluded walking paths around the facility. She handed out a map with these paths clearly identified.

Sister Spalding, a large, imposing woman with mostly gray hair, also provided schedule and location information on Masses, Lauds, Vespers and other events they were all welcome to attend, in silence of course. She emphasized that there was no smoking inside any building and added that the swimming pool had closed after the Labor Day weekend. When she asked if there were any questions, no one seemed to have the courage to talk, Orville included. "Very well," she concluded. "All this information is also provided on the desk in your room."

Orville's room was small, about 200 square feet he guessed, and sparsely furnished with a crucifix, a twin bed, a small desk with a lamp, an oval throw rug and a rather uncomfortable straight-backed wooden chair. There was also a sink with a small mirror but the shower and toilet were in a shared facility at the end of the hall. None of the doors to the rooms had locks. Thankfully, there was an inside bolt to secure the common bathroom when in use. Of course, there was no TV and no radio. There was also no air conditioning so Orville was very thankful he was there in late September when he opened the window and felt the cool breeze. With no TV, radio or internet accessibility, Orville quickly became very bored and wished he had brought something along to read. As soon as the sun had set, Orville went to bed.

On Thursday, Orville attended Mass and sat quietly through the meals trying to look as spiritual and peaceful as possible. In the afternoon, he went on a number of the recommended walks, none of which took him to the north where Bruno had suggested he should explore. He also got in his car and drove back to Shakespeare where he bought a few books and the latest "Economist" magazine. He fell asleep reading the magazine on Thursday evening.

After Mass and breakfast on Friday morning, Orville decided to head north and explore the areas Bruno had outlined. He took his special phone and pen with him just in case.

After a 30-minute walk he reached one of the cabins Bruno had circled on the map. It looked like it had been unoccupied for a few years. After reviewing Bruno's satellite map, he followed a small trail that led to another "target" Bruno had circled as a possible location where a hostage might be held. After a 20-minute hike through the woods he came upon a clearing with a cabin nestled on the edge of the woods on the far side. Kneeling behind bushes at the edge of the woods, he noticed a gravel road connected to the west end of the clearing and a gray truck parked in a carport which attached to a small shed just east of the cabin. The woods were so thick that the shed and carport weren't even visible in the satellite imagery Bruno had provided.

Orville stayed in the woods and circled to his right along the east side of the clearing until he was about 100 feet from the cabin. It was much larger than the unoccupied one he had scouted earlier, possibly a couple of bedrooms and maybe 1200 or so square feet. He made his way to a small window on the side of the shed and peered in. What he saw made his heart start racing: a black limousine!

Only then did he notice what looked to be a security camera mounted on the shed. He did not expect this at all and felt like a fool for being so careless. Maybe it wasn't pointed in the right direction to have observed his approach, he hoped? Then he noticed a second camera on the shed and yet another on the side of the cabin. A black limo and a cabin in the woods with security cameras positioned with overlapping fields of view! Jackpot!

Orville knew it was time to skedaddle but just as he was about to retreat into the woods the cabin door opened and a man with a bright red beard, wearing overalls and holding a shotgun appeared. Orville bent forward and froze behind a small bush. With no hesitation, the bearded man started walking directly toward where Orville crouched. When the man was about 20 feet away he stopped, raised the gun, pointed it directly at where Orville was hiding and said, "Now come on out with your hands in the air." Orville hesitated a few seconds.

"I mean right now you sonofabitch or I'll blow you and that little bush to fucking pieces!" the overalled man yelled.

Orville stood up and held his hands high. The man with the shotgun was close now and Orville saw that he was a very, very large man, around 6 and a half feet tall and certainly weighing well over 300 pounds. His red hair and matching beard were almost orange in color.

The giant directed him to lie face down with his hands clasped behind his head and Orville complied. He was patted down, blindfolded and shoved into the cabin, then onto a chair. After he was stripped down to his boxer shorts, his hands were tied behind his back and his legs were bound securely to the front legs of a chair.

After about 10 minutes, he heard another chair being dragged to somewhere just in front of him and a new male voice, different than the coarse raspy voice of the bearded giant, inquired softly.

"Well, sir, what exactly are you doing here?" the Voice asked.

"I'm on a retreat over at Peace Haven and just wanted a little exercise," Orville explained and although he tried to sound calm and confident, he sensed a slight tremor in his own voice. "What are you doing threatening me with a weapon and tying me up? You need to untie me now and let me go!" Orville insisted, trying again to sound both innocent and indignant.

The Voice chuckled softly. "Well, sir, you are really in no position to make such demands. You were trespassing on private property. You are well over one mile from the Motherhouse and far removed from any of the retreat's walking paths. You have a map of our property with this cabin circled in red. And you have some kind of fancy bat phone here too. You were clearly targeting us for some reason and I want to know that reason. So once again, I am asking you what are you doing here?"

The Voice was calm and measured with only the slightest hint of irritation. Orville thought it might be the voice of a black man. There was just something about the way he pronounced certain words that gave Orville that impression.

"I told you. I am here on a retreat and apparently got a little lost in the woods," Orville asserted again.

"Let me work over this lying sonofabitch," yelled the raspy voice from somewhere just behind Orville's left ear. He was so close that Orville felt the warmth of his breath and smelled the bourbon. "I'll get this little bastard to tell us the truth in no time at all."

"Stay cool, Red," the Voice in front of Orville commanded calmly. Over the next 30 minutes, this 2-man good cop, bad cop act continued. The Voice to the front speaking in calm, measured tones and repeating over and over again the same question as to Orville's purpose while "Red" paced behind Orville's chair periodically yelling his suggestions of water boarding, cattle prods and cigarette burns. Finally, the Voice took a new approach.

"Sir, we know who you are and why you are here. We need to know if you are here by yourself or if you are part of a team?" the Voice asked. Orville stuck to his retreat narrative and said that, of course, he was there by himself, as an individual just seeking some space for reflection.

After about an hour, Orville heard a door open and shut. The two men had stepped outside and they were talking. He couldn't quite make out what they were saying. Suddenly he heard Red's distinctive voice almost scream, "Well, what the fuck do you wanna do? Sister Spalding's gonna notice that he ain't there for dinner! He also probably checks in on that damn phone every day and whoever the fuck he calls will send in some serious muscle when the asshole doesn't phone home." The Voice responded but too softly to be understood.

"They'll be looking for him as early as tomorrow. He walked here and the bloodhounds will lead them to this cabin. We need to move him and the old man tonight," Red yelled.

Orville's hair stood on end. "The old man!" Could Horst Schwarz actually be here in the cabin with him? As he heard the cabin door start to open, Orville started yelling, "Horst, are you here? Horst? Horst?"

Just before a crushing blow landed on the left side of his head and sent both him and the chair crashing to the floor, Orville distinctly heard someone yell, "Yes, yes, this is Horst! Who are you?"

When he regained consciousness, he was sitting upright in the chair again. His jaw ached. The blindfold had been removed but his mouth had been taped shut. Sitting directly in front of him was a heavier, graying version of his childhood friend, Marty Sims.

"That's right, Sam. It's me, Marty," Sims purred softly. "Never expected to see you under these circumstances. Guess it's the same for you, huh? Anyway, when we heard a Mr. Sam Wright would be dropping in for a retreat and might visit our little cabin, I was shocked that my old teammate actually worked for a badass company like Acme. But the medical insurance card in your wallet sure enough says you are an Acme employee. I'd love to talk with you about how you ended up working for a criminal like Mr. Schwarz and we should have plenty of time for that later. I just can't understand how the altar boy I knew could now build such terrible machines that kill so many innocent people. Anyway, right now, we need to clear out of this cabin and we're really not very well set up for moving two people at once.

"Of course, Red here thinks we should just simplify things by killing you and setting fire to the limo with you inside. And he's right. Relocating just the old man would be much easier and you represent no additional leverage at all. But that's not what we're all about and the Mother Superior, Sister Mary Wilfred, would be very, very upset if anyone actually got hurt. And of course, you and I were friends once and that should count for something I guess."

Orville's mind was racing. How did they know he was coming? How could he be so stupid as to leave his Acme-provided insurance card in his wallet? More importantly, how was he going to alert Bruno? They had not arranged a periodic check-in and Bruno probably wouldn't worry about him for a few more days. He and Horst could be moved to a different state by that time. Now he wished that federal agencies were involved and not just some of Hannes' trusted friends.

Looking over his shoulder, Marty said, "Red, get me a pen and some paper. I need you to hand carry a short note over to Sister Mary Wilfred. We need to tell her what's happened and that we plan to leave at midnight tonight with the two hostages and move to the new location. I don't think she'll have any issues with the plan but you never know."

Red went to several places looking for something to write on without success and was getting frustrated when Marty pointed to some brown paper grocery bags in a corner and said, "Just bring me one of those bags and fetch me that nice pen we borrowed from my old pal."

"He might be your old pal but he's just an asshole trying to fuck things up as far as I'm concerned," Red said as he handed Marty the grocery bag and Bruno's very special pen. Orville watched as Marty pushed the end of the ballpoint pen and started to write.

Drones

EPILOGUE

About 30 minutes after Marty started to write his note, Bruno and a half dozen heavily armed men arrived at the cabin. Luckily, Red had quickly delivered the grocery bag note to the Mother Superior and received her approval. He had returned to the cabin only about 5 minutes before Bruno and the "SWAT" Team arrived. All the eggs were in one basket. It was a total tactical surprise. There was no shoot out, just a quick capitulation.

The federal government was not at all pleased that Schwarz's "private army" had operated without their knowledge and had resolved the kidnapping without their help. However, Horst's kidnapping had never been publicized so the government's embarrassment was limited and their reaction was very muted. Eventually, Martin Sims and Tom "Red" Mattingly were sentenced to 20-year prison terms. Two men in Colorado who had attempted to kidnap the GA Chairman were apprehended and sentenced to shorter prison terms. Sister Mary Wilfred was also sentenced to a long prison term but suffered a fatal heart attack a few hours after the verdict was read. No other nuns faced charges.

Horst Schwarz returned to work, if anything, even more driven than before the kidnapping to build his business empire and legacy. Orville quietly resumed his job as the Ares Program Manager at Red Rock. Unfortunately, Rock Bottom continued to interfere and make all substantive Program decisions. By December, the Ares Program was forced through a significant restructure because of major cost and schedule overruns. Orville found it impossible to hold himself accountable for the deteriorating contract performance. He had also heard rumors that Rock was telling Fred and Horst that the Program's problems were principally caused by Orville's lack of experience and familiarity with the "Acme way." Orville's frustrations mounted and in the spring of the following year, after exactly one year as an employee at Acme, he resigned. Hopalong Boyd accepted his resignation "with regret." Malibu replaced him immediately as the nominal Ares Program Manager.

Luscious and Orville resumed their dating as soon as he returned from Kentucky and their relationship immediately jumped from sweetly platonic to a very passionate, physical bonding: from first base to home plate with no stops at second or third. He avoided talking about his Kentucky adventure and she did not bring it up.

On Valentines Day, he asked her if she would marry him. She cried as she voluntarily confessed her part in a conspiracy with the Sisters of the Most Holy Cross and her long relationship with Sister Mary Wilfrid whom she had met long ago while a novitiate at a convent in Brazil. She told Orville that Sister Wilfrid had asked her to hire on with Acme to have someone "on the inside." At their request, she had provided the Mother Superior with the details of Mr. Schwarz's annual Lexington trip but said she didn't know about the kidnapping until after it occurred. By sheer coincidence, she was brought in to the CAT team. At that point she felt she was in too deep to back out. She also told Orville she had no idea that Mr. Schwarz was being held near the Motherhouse.

Deciding to "betray" Orville and tell Sister Mary Wilfrid that a Sam Wright at Acme had suspected a possible connection to the religious order and was going to snoop around the Motherhouse under the cover of attending a retreat there was an extremely painful decision. Luscious repeated that she didn't know where Horst was being held and that she didn't think there was any chance Orville would find Horst anywhere near the retreat, especially after her warning to Sister Mary Wilfrid.

At this point, she broke down completely and Orville wrapped his arms around her. He told her that Mr. Sims had told him they knew in advance he was coming to the retreat and he had concluded that she had to be the one who had warned them. He told her he fully understood her bind, and really didn't care. He wanted to spend his life with her regardless. However, he was very glad she had told him on her own. She said yes to his marriage proposal and they made wild, tearful love for hours that evening.

Lucia quit her job at Acme a few months after Orville resigned. Orville and Lucia were married that September at St James Catholic Church in Redondo Beach with both families in full attendance. Only Malibu attended from Acme. During an extended honeymoon in Brazil, Orville interviewed with the aerospace company, Embraer. Orville was hired by Embraer and they moved to Sao Jose dos Campos in the state of Sao Paulo later that winter. Orville and Lucia had the first of their three children, all boys, the following year.

Late the same year that Orville resigned, the government terminated the Ares and Daedallus contracts for poor performance. "Hopalong" Boyd tried to get Fred and Horst to fire Rock Bottom but they were unwilling to do so and Boyd retired in disgust. Fred Gallop replaced "Hopalong" as

President and Siggy was promoted to serve as Fred's deputy, the new number 2. With Rock still in position as the VP of Programs, Malibu decided he had had enough. He resigned and went back to work for Northrop.

Two years later, the government awarded a new highly classified prime contract to Boeing on a sole source basis. The effort was essentially to continue the full-scale development efforts previously terminated. Boeing subcontracted some work to Acme that represented only about 15 percent of the total contract value.

One year after the contract award, the Schwarz family sold Acme Aviation to the Boeing Company. Fred Gallop retired and was replaced by an experienced Boeing executive who quickly understood they could not achieve the needed cultural transformation without "breaking some eggs." Jim "Rock" Bottom was pushed into retirement and several other senior executives were fired for cause just 6 months after the acquisition.

Drones

ABOUT THE AUTHOR

"Porter Drucker" is a pseudonym of the shy author, an experienced and well-traveled aerospace executive, who prefers to remain hidden behind the curtain of a *nom de plume*.